When
Katie
Wakes

DOUBLEDAY ⚓ NEW YORK LONDON TORONTO SYDNEY AUCKLAND

When Katie Wakes

a memoir

Connie May Fowler

PUBLISHED BY DOUBLEDAY
a division of Random House, Inc.
1540 Broadway, New York, New York 10036

DOUBLEDAY and the portrayal of an anchor with a dolphin
are trademarks of Doubleday, a division of Random House, Inc.

Library of Congress Cataloging-in-Publication Data
Fowler, Connie May.
When Katie wakes: a memoir / by Connie May Fowler.—1st ed.
p.   cm.
1. Fowler, Connie May—Childhood and youth.   2. Novelists, American—20th
century—Biography.   3. Abused children—Services for—Florida.
4. Women dog owners—Florida—Biography.   5. Fowler, Connie May—
Relations with men.   6. Abused women—Services for—Florida.   7. Abused
children—Florida—Biography.   8. Abused women—Florida—Biography.
9. Labrador retriever.   I. Title.
PS3556.O8265 Z477   2002
813' .54—dc21
2001037165

ISBN 0-385-50201-X
PRINTED IN THE UNITED STATES OF AMERICA
January 2002

First Edition

Designed by Mauna Eichner

For Mika and Katie
and for the women unable to find a pathway out
then, now, and always

Acknowledgments

IT'S IMPOSSIBLE for me to thank the many people who have—knowingly or not—shepherded me to where I stand today. So I humbly offer this list—incomplete in scope and gratitude—of a few special people and one dog. I believe that without them, this book would never have been written.

Deb Futter and Joy Harris, two avenging angels, whose passion for the story and truth never wavers.

Mika Fowler, my dear husband, best friend, confidant, and critic, whose strength, wisdom, and humor forever carry me out of the past and into a life I love.

Dr. David Kahn, whose friendship and advice buoyed me during some of the most trying times in the writing of this book.

Dale Copans-Astrand and Dr. Per Astrand, dear friends whose laughter, grand food, and infectious cheer are always good medicine.

Kelly Otte, a warrior princess if ever there was one,

whose dedication to battered women is unparalleled and whose friendship and erudite advice helped me to heal and to find the strength to tell the truth.

Rhonda and Robert Heins, wonderful friends who have selflessly allowed me to experience what life is like with good parents.

Heidi Swanson, a friend of many gifts, who transforms chaos into order with a magician's flair.

Pamela Ball, whose comments regarding a few pages written long ago became my compass.

Heather Nicoll and George Pequignot, two sweet souls to whom Mika and I are forever grateful. Thank you for introducing us. Thank you for casting a light on the pathway out.

Jerry Morgan, whose friendship, then and now, exceeds all expectations.

Deborah Bax Freeland, whose intellect, humor, and life experience is both beautiful and terrifying and binds us forever as sisters.

My mother's children—Deidre Hankins and Jimmy Friend—whose pain is only hinted at in these pages and whose strength of character and joy have always inspired me.

My father's children—Aubrey May and Hendra Conrad— beacons in the dark fog of our past and today cherished siblings.

My parents—Henry and Lenore May—whose tragic lives and unintentional sins never extinguished their children's love for them.

Miss Vivian, Olga Barnes, Patty Davis, Kathy Clark, Scott

Morse, Randall King, Johnny Mae Marshall, Dr. Stephen Meats, Dr. Mark Lono, and Carolyn Doty—all dear people whose generous gifts of friendship and guidance led me forward.

Lloyd Kramer, Kate Forte, and Oprah Winfrey, whose belief in my story enabled me to think of myself in a new and positive light.

The many good folks at Doubleday, including Anne Merrow and Amy King, whose diligence and talent are deeply appreciated.

And of course there is Katie, whose life inspired this book. You are missed.

When
Katie
Wakes

Brother John, can you see the hopeless daughters,
standing there with broken wings?

DANIEL LANOIS, "THE MAKER"

Prologue

THIS MAN I SHARE A LIFE WITH—the one who beat me last night, the one who is thirty years my senior and unemployed—has pocketed the spare change off the dresser and pilfered a twenty out of my wallet and headed over to Salina's, a bar down the street, to get tanked up.

I support the two of us with my weekly earnings as a hostess and bartender at Bennigan's. I know this is insane, but right now I haven't the resources or mental gumption to leave. For all intents and purposes, I'm all he has. I provide shelter and food and make his car payment. He drives a slick silver Audi with fancy hubcaps that have the heft and glint of money.

I am not proud of my situation. I am twenty-six years old and have a college degree. I should be out there busting my butt in the job market, hustling for dollars and influence. After all, what did *Newsweek* dub 1984—the "Year of the Yuppie"? Where is my ambition? My confidence? English lit isn't the finest degree to have—to get ahead these days you need an MBA—but I can string sentences together. I can tell a story. I used to be able to do things. I used to be able to look a challenge in the eye and say, "Go for it." But not anymore.

And that's where he comes in. He promised to make me into somebody. The first time we spoke when it was just the two of us, he sat at the bar at Bennigan's nursing a scotch and soda and said, "You need me, kid. I'll show you the ropes. It's your choice."

He twirled his cigarette lighter on the smooth surface of the bar as if we were playing spin the bottle. He slapped his palm on top of it, and when he lifted his hand the ignition end was pointing in my direction.

"You wanna play? It's all up to you, baby."

Goddamn it, I wanted to. I wanted someone who was strong and capable—someone I could respect—to help me pull my life together. I had prayed for someone like him to come along. After Mama died, I didn't have anyone in the world to offer me direction. And here he sat, the answer to my prayers—a big shot in town, tall and tan and silver-haired and famous.

"Okay," I said as I poured him another scotch—this time, top-shelf—and I poured it long, raising the bottle high into the air. "I'll play."

Then I added, with far less bravado, staring down into the well, "I know I need help."

His method of schooling me is harsh, unkind even. And though I resent it, I cannot dissolve the feeling that I have brought this curse upon myself, that I was born helpless and ignorant, and that he is simply fulfilling a cosmic will.

For instance, just last night he accused me again of being a stupid, ungrateful cunt. My mind, as it always does in the heat of this accusation, split in half. In a single instant, one side of my brain thought, *Yes, you're absolutely right. I deserve your wrath. Go ahead. Beat me. Please. Lay bare my shame.*

But the other side shouted, *Ungrateful for what? Doing your laundry? Paying your bills? Cooking your meals?*

This little internal battle, of course, was fought silently. I have learned to disengage. To take it all in and carry the rage deep inside so that no one sees the real me. Sometimes, in the midst of my silence, I feel as if my voice has been exiled to a land beyond speech, as if I'm stumbling through a hazy, booze-choked nightmare of consonants, vowels, language.

His charge that I'm stupid resonates far deeper than even he suspects. I've said it myself about battered women I've known along the way: "Why doesn't she just leave?" That's the advice du jour, what most any person would say if I told them about my situation, which I have not done. Being a battered woman is my secret. I cannot tell even my sister because I fear the judgment. To announce my situation is to proclaim that I have failed: Here I am, doing what I always pledged I would never do, walking in my mother's footsteps.

But I digress. About this stupidity charge, our lives exist on many levels, some seen and others submerged far beyond our reach. On the surface, *I am* stupid, weak, helpless. But way down deep, in the sweet, private darkness of my interior life, I am a strong woman with a plan. My animal instincts are in overdrive, confounding rote, worn-out judgments.

For instance, I plot how to stay alive. Don't run out of coffee. Keep his shirts starched and properly organized, white to blue to black, and hung on silk padded hangers. Iron the sheets. Never contradict him. Laugh with him, not at him, remembering you have no control over his perception. When he doesn't come home for three days, do not press him about where he has been. And when he hits you, anticipate it. Head for the door. Know where your keys are. Always have a private stash of money—even if it's only a few dollars. Keep your car gassed up. It's your way out. Your only way out.

Here, in the cool shadows of my subterranean world, I mull over the practical considerations of freedom. The fact that I am not keen on being homeless. And that despite my best efforts to save enough for a deposit on a new place, he runs through my money with sleight-of-hand speed. And when I act recklessly—when my plans for a way out seep into the jumbled chaos of my exterior life—he senses it and grows more violent. I must approach freedom with the slow, deliberate movements of a lover's waltz. But the beat keeps changing. And I'm a lousy dancer.

What I'm trying to say is this: Staying does not mean that I'm not also in the process of leaving. Staying means I am conserving my energy. Staying means I am using my few clearheaded moments to plan my exit. Staying means I am figuring out how to remain alive for the long haul. Staying is an amazing feat of drowning; surviving the moment takes every speck of intellect and will I can gather. But it's a temporary condition. I will break the surface.

But hold on. It gets worse. Comical, even. You see, despite the fact that we sleep in the same bed, sex isn't an issue since testicular cancer forever altered the stuff between his legs. He claims he was walking from Florida to California because he had no money (imagine that!), and his girlfriend, who'd moved to L.A. after their breakup, finds herself in the family way. What's a fella to do? He has to get to California by hook or crook and announce to the world that he's a stand-up daddy. So there he is, strolling beside a golf course somewhere in Alabama, walking across America in order to be with his unborn baby, when—whack!—an errant golf ball slams full speed into, well, his balls. Can God aim or what? He spends the rest of the afternoon and night doubled over under the shade of a picnic table. That's how he got the cancer. So he says.

A year ago he hosted his own talk shows: weekly TV, daily radio. Some people called him the "King of Tampa Bay." His face was everywhere. Even on billboards. He loomed over the rest of us Reagan-era peons, gazing down at our hapless souls like Fitzgerald's Dr. Eckleburg, as we squandered our Me Generation lives beneath his unblinking three-foot gaze, lemmings unable to reach the cliff's edge, trapped in a never-abating traffic jam, lulled or annoyed by his carefully calibrated radio voice.

He is a man in love with his addictions: cocaine, liquor, and younger women (you know, all razzle and dazzle but he can't make the pocket). These addictions combined with a laser-sharp knack for enemy making are the cornerstones of his downfall. The King of Tampa Bay has been exiled to the ranks of the unemployed, and no one really cares. In the Tampa–St. Petersburg media meat market, he is a leper. The billboards are all gone and so is his voice. It no longer steals its way along the invisible airwaves, tricking us into blind complacency simply through the power of those honey-toned, aged-in-a-sherry-cask intonations.

The pisser is, he is not missed. There was no public outcry when he got canned. People grow tired of kings and gods, you know. And because, before ever landing on our Gulf shores, he had napalmed his career in other markets, Florida was his last chance. And he blew it. So he is, it appears, a man without options.

Maybe that's why last night, when I asked him if he wanted anything to eat, he rabbit-kicked me from his throne in front of the TV, hitting me square in the stomach, knocking me onto the pine floor, and then kicking me repeatedly as I crawled toward the kitchen, a safe place because I can latch its door from the inside. His blows were rhythmic. One, two, three—kick! One, two, three—kick! One, two, three—kick! We must have looked like a sadistic version of Fred and Ginger. Right before I made it into the temporary safety of my kitchen, he spit on me. I felt his saliva, wet and cold, through the light weave of my cotton shirt.

And maybe this situation I find myself in—being a battered woman (as were my mother, grandmother, and great-grandmother), supporting a man who is old enough to be my father, desiring a better life for myself but not recognizing the path—is why I am barreling down Gunn Highway in my used heap of a car (a four-door red Torino with a three-fifty Cleveland engine and shot ball-joints), praying that I put enough water in my radiator to get me to my destination and back, consciously looking for a dirt road in the middle of an orange grove, but unconsciously seeking our most basic need as human souls: love, abiding and nonjudgmental.

"You'll see a fence post with a beer can nailed to it."

Those were my directions.

And this is where I'll find my dog.

.   .   .

SHE IS HIDING UNDER a blue tarpaulin. Her siblings, all tan and brown, run and hop, nipping at each other, uncaring whether I choose them or not. They have a good life. They live outside and have sticks to play with. If it rains, they seek shelter under the house. Shade is there, too. And so is Mama. Mama with all that milk. But she's drying up, and these long-boned, orange-grove Crackers know it. In fact, she doesn't look very healthy at all.

Skin and bones and skin and bones. Where do you run to when you're nothing but skin and bones!

"The paper said you had black Lab puppies."

"We do." He points at the tarpaulin. "She's over there."

I look at the lone black pup and then back at the Cracker with his sky-colored eyes and sunburned face. Two barefoot boys, maybe three and five, chase the pups and giggle wildly each time they bait one into a game of tug.

"Their daddy is a Lab. That there is the mama. She's a shepherd. We only got one black one."

He smiles, as if her rarity in this litter makes her extra special, and I wonder two things. In the classified ad, why did they credit only the father's bloodline? Especially since five of the six puppies bear no resemblance to their Labrador side. And why isn't the black puppy playing with her siblings? Is she sick? Hurt? An outcast based on color? Size? Temperament?

"Hey, sweetie," I say to her from across the yard.

I approach slowly and kneel beside her. "How are you, little bit?" I ask, trying to make my voice comforting, as though a gentle nature is something all humans possess.

A star-shaped patch of white gleams on her chest. Other than that, she is tip-to-toe black. I offer her my hand. She looks at me warily and then averts her gaze. I take her into my arms. At my touch, she tenses. I understand from both the cautious posture of her eyes and the rigid trembling of her body that this dog, just weeks old, knows about mistreatment. She begins to whimper. Low, baleful, constant.

"It's okay, baby, yes, everything is gonna be all right."

I hear the Cracker say, "Looks like a keeper to me!" and he laughs loudly. It's a laugh made fat with good-ol'-boy intentions.

"Has she seen a vet?" I can see from her distended belly that she's wormy.

"Nah. I thought I'd leave that up to whoever is lucky enough to take her home. Besides, seeings how we ain't got room for no more dogs, we're probably just gonna croaker-sack whichever ones are left past this weekend. Back in the creek, you know." He nods toward a slow-moving rivulet of brown water that flows at the edge of a cane-break, sucks his teeth, and then yells toward the house, "Gracie, get me a beer." He looks at me. Slow. Up and down. "You want one?"

I shake my head no, flushed with rage, unable to match his blatant gaze. I feel his violence. It is palpable in each tremor of this puppy's underfed body.

"She's mine. I'm going to take her," I hear myself say as I ferry the dog to the car.

The older of the two boys is stomping, yelling, "Bye-bye!" The pups are scattering out of his path. His brother snags one by the scruff and carries it through the dirt as if it's a rag doll.

The Cracker yells, "You sure you want only one?"

Gracie steps onto the porch. She is as thin as the shepherd dog. I don't know if she's the Cracker's daughter or wife. He takes the beer from her and slaps her fanny. She slumps on the porch steps, arms folded in front of her, and stares at the dirt.

I am unbelievably grateful when the engine, after three sputtering tries, finally cranks.

My new dog is curled on the seat beside me, a tiny black curlicue, frightened and not understanding. As we travel out of the grove—even as my car shakes violently, banging along on its nearly nonexistent ball joints—I tell her, over and over, my hand stroking the bony ridge of her back, "I'm gonna take good care of you."

. . .

I NAME HER KATELAND, after Caitlin Costello Price in the movie *The Verdict*. I identify with Caitlin. She's long-suffering, and even though it takes forever, she finally does the right thing and testifies.

. . .

WHEN I TELL the receptionist at the vet's office how to spell Katie's name, I don't intentionally mess it up. But once I realize my error, I feel no compulsion to fix it. Katie doesn't care how her name is spelled.

. . .

SHE IS A KIND DOG. She sleeps with me, on my side of the bed, right up against my belly. Every night before dozing off, she licks my hand. When the lights are out, I cannot see her. But I cling to her. And I think, she to me.

. . .

YOU PICK HER UP by her scruff and inspect her as if you are an animal know-it-all.

"Don't handle her like that," I say.

You measure your words evenly, as if speaking to a child who is hopelessly dense. "That's the way it's done."

"No, it's not."

"Jesus, Connie, my father was a vet. I know what I'm doing."

You set her down and then try to force open her jaws. She squirms out of your grip. Quickly, I pick her up and hold her to my chest. She's trembling as much as on the day I brought her home.

You look over my head and say—that old arrogance shining through—"I'll have her trained in no time."

"I mean it, leave her alone."

And in my mind I'm saying, *You motherfucker. You motherfucker.*

You look at me with a bored, superior gaze and, for the first time in months, I stare right back, certain that if you hurt this dog I will kill you.

.   .   .

I AM FIXING SUPPER. Katie lies on the floor, ever-watchful for any morsel I might toss her way. I spice the ground beef (I have given up my vegetarian ways, living with you). Salt, pepper, garlic powder, Worcestershire, and finely chopped onions. I mix it together with my bare hands, the raw meat cold and bloody against my skin.

You have been missing in action since about three yesterday afternoon. Still, here I am, preparing an evening meal, as if this domestic ritual will set my world straight. I have fantasies, like maybe you've been killed in a car crash, and I don't know whether to be upset or joyous. Each time a car slows in front of the apartment I peer out the window, hoping against all odds that it is you returning home.

Maybe I'll call the sheriff. Maybe I'll say, "Are there any accident reports involving a slick silver Audi driven by a drunk?"

Why should I fear being abandoned by you? I should hope and pray that you're gone for good. I slap the meat into patties and try to remember how long my mama has been dead. Two, three years? I can't recall. Same with Daddy. People ask, "How old were you when he died?" and I shrug my shoulders.

"I'm not sure. Little."

And they look at me as if I were a loon for not pinning down how old he was, how old I was, how old Mama was.

Maybe I can't remember because the numbers frighten me. They are cold, unchangeable. The opposite, I hope, of life.

. . .

HERE'S A MEMORY TO CHOKE ON:

I'm little. How many years I am slips around me. Sometimes I grab it tight, sometimes it skitters away. Five? Five and a half? Maybe even six. One, two, three, four, five, six. I can count that far! Even to ten but I don't feel like it. Oh well, doesn't matter, I'll figure everything out later, on my fingers.

I have on a decent outfit—a new shorts set my mama sewed for me. It's blue with tiny yellow rocket ships zooming between all white stars. Mama can sew good, except she makes me thread her needles 'cause she says she's blind as a bat. I've got my doll with me. She's sitting beside me in the back seat of the Rambler. A little smile on her face. She's perfect. I like her white underwear.

Mama is driving and smoking and cussing Daddy. Deedee is riding shotgun. That's what Mama calls it. She ain't got no gun, though. She's just helping Mama find Daddy's car. She's a big priss, sitting up front, peering out her window, acting like she's better than me just 'cause Mama told her that one day she'd let her shave her legs.

My doll has good legs. If she were real, she'd end up marrying a leg man. I stretch mine out. They're freckled from the sun. My toes ain't got no paint on 'em, either. When I get big, I probably won't be attracting no leg men. But how about—

"Constance Anita May, get your goddamned feet off the back of my seat before I smack you!"

I do as I'm told, but I'm not happy about it. Mama is a meanie. I hate her! I pick up my doll and whisper right in her face, "I weren't hurting nobody."

Mama slows the car and I stretch my neck to see out the window. There's a pretty sign up there. Words written in diamonds.

"There it is!" Deedee says as if she's just won a treasure hunt.

"Bingo!" Mama stops right in front of the bar, but she keeps the car running. "Connie, go in there and get that son-of-a-bitch father of yours."

I don't want to go. I don't like the way those drinkers look at me. They cuss a lot. Bars stink and floozies live there. Mama said so.

Mama turns around, her hand raised, her green eyes shifting back and forth—a sure sign she's about to blow. "What did I just tell you!"

I leave my doll in the car. She'll probably thank me for it later.

There ain't no ladies in here. Just men, drinking, laughing, playing pool. And a lot of smoking. I stand right inside the door. I don't move. I just look around. With my eyes. Nobody has seen me. Maybe I'm invisible. I like that jukebox over there. It's lit up. Yellow. Red. Green. I gotta pee. Bad. I don't know where my daddy is. Maybe that weren't his car. Maybe Mama was wrong.

I look with just my eyes one more time. Pool games. Tables. That back room through all this smoke. Maybe this is Hell, right here where I'm standing. Mama says her grandma believed in Hell on earth. The bar. It's crowded. Maybe he's down on the end and that's why I don't see him.

"Henry!"

That's my daddy's name! The bartender with his belly floating like a balloon above his pants. He said it.

My daddy swings around on his barstool. "Hey, sunshine!" He's grinning like a jack-o'-lantern. No wonder I couldn't see him. His back was to me. "Come here. Don't be scared. Nobody's gonna bite."

I inch on over to him. I know about inchworms. They're everywhere. Sometimes I let them crawl through my arm hairs. Daddy seems real happy to see me. He lifts me onto his lap and introduces me to his buddies.

"This is my baby girl. Ain't she the pertiest thing you ever did see!"

They all say yep and the bartender reaches over with his ham-sized paw and shakes my hair. I press my face against Daddy's shirt. It smells like starch and sweat. Mama's gonna claim that's the stink of women and liquor.

"What do you want?" Daddy asks. "Cherry Coke? Pickled egg? How about a Slim Jim, sunshine?"

I shake my head no. I try to make him understand. I do my serious face, the I-mean-business face. "Mama's waiting out in the car."

"She is!" Daddy seems real surprised. Does he think I walked here? "Well, what's she doing out there?" He tosses some paper money on the bar. "Let's go get her. Later, boys," he says.

I'm too big to be carried, but Daddy don't pay that any mind. To tell the truth, I kinda like it. Maybe these bar fellas think I'm some paralyzed child—all weak and pale and pretty like my doll—and Daddy's being the hero, walking us straight out of Hell.

. . .

I FLATTEN OUT the patties with the palm of my hand and hear Mama's voice, clear, like a razor shining in a pool of light. *"Your father beat me so bad my face looked like ground beef."* I don't know what to do with that information, other than mourn. I pour a couple of tablespoons of oil in the pan and watch as it spreads, thinned by the heat. She didn't always run after him. Sometimes she stayed home, claiming the kitchen table as her territory, fretting, smoking, ruminating, turning her lighter over and over in her hand just as if she were saying the rosary.

On those nights I knew to steer clear. I might sit in the living room, playing jacks, well out of slapping range, spying on her out of the corner of my eye. And I would try to make myself small, so small I wouldn't even be an itch in her imagination. I would rock back and forth, saying to myself, "Disappear, disappear, disappear." But getting rid of flesh and blood isn't easy.

"Deidre Katherine, Constance Anita, get your asses in the kitchen now!

We would run double-time and I would think about Gomer Pyle and I would understand deep in my belly that patience was not my mama's strong suit.

"Stand up straight! Put your shoulders back. When will you girls stop slumping?" Then, as if to punctuate her sudden decisiveness, she'd rap her knuckles on the kitchen table and say, "That's it. I'm calling the police."

"No!"

"Why not?"

"They might put us in jail!" I'd say, but the words would come out jumbled, all in the wrong order and full of stutters.

Didn't matter. Mama understood. "You stupid child, they will not. For Christ's sakes, your daddy could be lying dead in a ditch somewhere. And us just sitting here! Do you want that? Huh? Answer me!"

"No, ma'am."

"Then pull that phone over here."

. . .

WHAT GAIN, what natural realignment of good and evil, could possibly result from calling the police? Daddy was one of theirs. A retired St. Augustine cop. They loved Daddy. He was their friend. Their drinking buddy. Their co-conspirator in all manner of chicanery.

And what if they were of a mind to help a frantic woman alone with two kids? Were there any domestic violence hot-lines? Any social services? Any battered women's shelters? Any judges who didn't believe in the God-given right of the man of the house to exert his masculine will even if that will manifested itself as neglect and abuse?

No.

None of those things existed.

I guess the world was a different place.

. . .

KATIE STAMPS HER FEET. She is an impatient dog when it comes to food.

"Do you want some hamburger, baby? Okay, it'll be just a second. Let Mama cook one."

The phone book is right there in the corner, next to the cookie jar that's shaped like an apple. What harm could a phone call do? Maybe you really are in serious trouble. I place the patty in the center of the frying pan. The hot oil hisses and spatters. Mama was quick to call the cops if she couldn't find Daddy. But she wasn't so quick to phone them after a beating. Why should she have bothered? Black eyes and busted lips settled everything. Besides, it wasn't against the law to beat your wife. Beat her but don't kill her, that was law enforcement's advice. And neighbors sure weren't going to help: That's a private matter between a man and a woman. Do not interfere.

I slip my spatula under the patty and turn it over. I see those cops with their smart-assed grins gaining our front steps, laughing at a joke that may well have been at our expense. I shut my eyes against the truth: They never helped us. I wished she had never called them. I wish the past wasn't real, that the voices that haunt me in my waking and sleeping hours were make-believe.

.   .   .

"Mama! The cops are here!"

"We'll do what we can, Lee. He's probably just out having a

few drinks, blowing off some steam. . . . Now, Lee, you need to calm down."

"Henry, put down the gun, you're scaring the children."

"I'm gonna blow my fucking brains out!"

"I can't take anymore!"

"Deedee, Daddy's got a gun!"

"You useless son of a bitch. I rue the day I ever met you!"

"I'm going to take the girls so far away you'll never see them again, you no good lying bastard!"

"She asked for it."

"She goaded him on."

"That ought to teach him a lesson."

"It's none of our business."

"A man can only take so much."

"You can't act this way. He's the father of your children. Now go in there and apologize."

"Mama, we can't ride in that cop car. Everybody will think I did something wrong!"

"Get in there, you little bitch! Don't you dare fight me!"

"Your no good father busted my goddamned teeth!"

"Deedee, come quick! Mama's hurt bad."

. . .

"KATIE, how about some meat, little girl?"

I break off a piece of burger and offer it to her. She grins before eating it as if she can't believe her good fortune. Her smile makes me laugh. I've never known a smiling dog before. Not like this. She pulls back her doggy lips, exposing her gums and teeth, and her nose ever so slightly wrinkles.

"Where do you think he is, Katie? What do you think we should do?"

She looks at me as if she's actually considering my dilemma. I feed her more of the burger. Then she lies down and closes her eyes.

So much for asking your dog for advice. I wash my hands, wipe them on my shirt, and reach for the phone book. What's wrong with filing a missing-person's report? I mean, technically you are missing. In fact, maybe you're dead. Maybe you got robbed and murdered. Or maybe someone thought you were a fat cat with that fancy car and kidnapped you. Maybe I'd be doing you a favor, teaching you a lesson.

And maybe I'm just like my mama. I mean, here I stand, staring down at the phone book, which I've set next to the plate of raw beef that needs to be put in the fridge, thinking about calling the police to find your missing ass. And, I realize, that just like her, I never reach for the phone after a beating. Never. I don't have any confidence that I'd be treated like the wronged instead of the wrongdoer. Your son is a sheriff in this county. And though it's the Reagan eighties and I hear things have changed, I can't be sure. I can't take the chance. If you beat me and get away with it even after I've called the police, there would be no stopping you.

Besides, you'd figure out a way to make it my fault. You'd

come out on top, a patient and good man helping out a dis-turbed young girl.

I'm not ready yet for that brand of humiliation.

. . .

THE HAMBURGER PATTIES are in the fridge covered in foil, and Katie and I are sitting outside, listening to the cicadas, waiting for you. I know you've got women on both sides of the bay, which is sort of laughable given your sexual prowess. I suppose ladies enjoy being wined and dined without having to put out. Plus, I'm sure you promise them the moon. Be-cause the aura of celebrity still clings to you ever so slightly, they believe your lies.

I believe you. When you tell me you'll turn me into a writer, that we'll pen movies together and live in Hollywood, my foolish hopefulness gushes like an opened vein.

When you say, "You've got the talent but not any dis-cipline. That's what I'm going to give you. Stick with me, kid, and I'll turn you into something," my heart shouts, *Yes! Yes! Yes!*

When you promise me we'll make so much money that I will be able to get my teeth fixed—these horrible teeth that don't fit into the small space of my mouth; these fucking teeth that spill out all over my face—I know I will do anything, endure anything, to make your promise come true.

Goddamn you to hell. I am going to pull a Mama. I'm

going to get in my Torino and find you. You'll be sorry you ever treated me this way.

I start to cry, both out of self-pity and because my gut tells me I have no choice but to repeat my mama's pathetic sins.

Katie nudges me with her cold nose. I pat her head and then lift her onto my lap. She alternately licks my tears and nuzzles her face against my neck. She is being gently persistent. Does this little spirit who came into my life barely a month ago sense my sadness?

Without a doubt, yes. She is trying to make me feel better. And she is succeeding. What a strange sensation— affection showered without strings. I'm not sure what to make of this. Or what to do next.

I whisper, "You are such a good dog. Yes, you are."

She gazes at me as if grateful for the compliment. There is no reason for me to doubt the purity of her response. She is enjoying the attention I am giving her. But she is also healing me. Only people who are blindly arrogant would dismiss as folly what is happening between the two of us.

I thank Katie for licking away my tears. I rub behind her ears. She seems to really like this. She cocks her head from side to side, pressing gently, following the motion of my hands. The next thing I know, I'm singing to her, an old ditty my Mama used to hum to me.

"K-K-K-Katie! K-K-K-Katie!"

But I change it from a human to a canine love song.

"You're the only d-d-d-dog that I adore! . . ."

I do not feel foolish singing a song to my dog. The kindness, the silliness of it, liberates me. I can't sing worth a damn and she doesn't care. It's the gesture she appreciates; I think it makes her feel special.

So I sing it to her again. Over and over. Sometimes softly. Sometimes raucously. Always off-key. Until the air turns cool with the rising of the moon.

.   .   .

KATIE AND I are in bed. She is snoring. I am staring at the ceiling, imagining amorphous shapes in the dark, obsessing over who you might be with tonight. The dye-job with the Tammy Faye eyes, or the hippie girl from the radio station, or maybe someone you picked up at a bar, someone I don't know, will never know, someone who can give you things: money, confidence, a job. Someone so kind you will never beat her or call her names. Someone who offers you mortal salvation or at least a way to pay the rent.

I am not thinking straight. Maybe that's one of the reasons you take off for days at a time. You know it keeps me rattled. As long as I'm agitated, unable to make rational decisions, you maintain the upper hand. Yes, even when you are not home, you are controlling me.

Have I given you this control? Or did you simply take it?

I don't know. The answer is buried somewhere, deep

in all this confusion, deep in the open sore that is my childhood.

Ours was a family life composed of smoke and mirrors, deception and shame. No one knew that Lee May beat her children. No one knew about her verbal assaults. No one knew she was an alcoholic—not even her three kids. No one knew she had been a battered woman and an abused child. No one knew when our electricity was turned off. No one knew about our humiliating trips to the pawn shop. No one knew about the many times one of us needed to see a doctor but couldn't afford it, so Mama resorted to her desperate cure-all: She forced us to eat Vicks. The roaches and vermin, the perpetual robbing Peter to pay Paul (one of Mama's favorite expressions), the anger and self-revulsion—all of this was hidden behind a scrim of practiced smiles and overachievement.

Yes, to the world we appeared admirable. Poignant, even. Mama was a widow raising two fine girls all by herself. She had a third child, a son, who lived up north, who was putting himself through college, and who sent money home from time to time because she had raised him right.

That's all anyone knew. And perhaps that's all they wanted to know. Because we were good examples. We were proof that poor people didn't have to behave like white trash. We showed the outside world what they wanted to see. The truth about child abuse and domestic violence and poverty and alcoholism is messy. It makes people uncomfortable. We were trying to enter their world. Honesty would have caused them to slam shut the door.

Besides, speaking the truth was completely impossible. Jimmy, Deidre, and I could not tattle on Mama. It's not in children's nature to betray their parents. She was God. We could not suffer her wrath any more than we already did. We could not bear the shame or the responsibility. The more she raged, the more we blamed ourselves. It is a cruel trick of the soul, but as our self-disgust grew so did our love for her. Perhaps, in some naive, fundamental way, we understood her anger and venom to be further evidence of her pain.

So the suffering must remain hidden behind a wall of silence. See, words are powerful. So very, very powerful. Even sister to sister and sister to brother, we never whispered the truth. This was not a case of denial. We each privately understood that we were in deep shit. We simply couldn't discuss it. Verbal acknowledgment even among ourselves was an act of betrayal. And we preferred to nurse our shame privately.

But let's get back to the business of being an overachiever. Deidre and I would have never dared be anything other than exemplary students. Straight A's. Honor clubs. Scholarships. Mama insisted on A's. B's made her crazy. Everything made her crazy.

Who did Mama curse, what damnations filled her sodden brain, as she, a widow, stood at that tiny trailer stove stirring the same mix of beans and celery and onions day after day, worrying about her health and our health and all the bills and wanting desperately for our future to have nothing in common with her past or present, watching the rich soup eventually thin into a watery broth?

What was Mama supposed to do? Get a job? Knocked out teeth and a nose misshapen from being broken narrows the old employment opportunities.

And didn't she say, "I want to stay home and watch my goddamned girls," and, "I can't leave two girls alone at night while I go work at 7-Eleven," and, "I wish God would strike me dead and put me out of my misery"?

Weren't her dreams for us admirable? Her behavior sacrificial? Saintly, even?

Think of it this way: Her delivery lacked grace but her message was well-intentioned.

But do good intentions carry equal weight with the damage inflicted by meanness?

The truth is, Deidre and I were so miserable at home that we would do anything to stay away from Mama. Even succeed. We sought refuge in books and school work and after-school clubs. We were, for Christ's sake, baton twirlers. But so much more! Latin Club. Spanish Club. Newspaper. Literary magazine. Beta Club. National Honor Society. Y-Teens. Join everything. Say yes to any club, staff, or committee that will have you.

My sister was beautiful. And smart. She was head majorette. She had boyfriends and a good figure and a perfect four-corner smile. She hid everything behind that smile. All of her heartache, anger, confusion, and contempt lingered just beyond sight. She was a perfectionist. The condition of her fingers was the only hint that her perfection was masking some sort of deep-seated sadness. She incessantly chewed on her nails until her skin was raw and her fingers bled.

As for me, I hid my mania behind books. Without them I would not have survived my childhood. In a universe fueled by booze and violence and poverty, books gave me a reason to believe that beyond the pale of my experience a parallel world awaited, a world where kindness outstripped cruelty. If I could just hang on long enough to find it. *Nellie Bly, Girl Reporter.* She succeeded. She took New York City by storm. And what about the family in *Strawberry Girl*? They were poor. They didn't live in a place much better than ours. But there was love in that household.

Yes, I soaked up words. I inhaled books. And when Mama's hurt and anger and pain manifested itself in a barrage of violence aimed at my sister and me, I grew hysterical, convinced that each word I uttered might provoke another beating. My words issued forth in a panicked torrent. When I tried to slow down, the sounds careened into an endless stutter.

Teachers said I had a speech impediment. Kids made fun of me.

"You're lying! You're stuttering! Stutterer! Liar! Stutterer! Liar!"

"I-I-I-I am not a l-l-l-liar!"

I insisted on my honesty over and over in a wailing stutter punctuated by flailing fists and swinging hair, my face knotted with rage.

So I became silent. And I read. And I listened. And all those words attached themselves to the insides of my veins and arteries and bones. And I began to write. And write. And write.

In school, my teachers praised me. Slowly, after a stint with a speech therapist, I started speaking again. And didn't my writing instructors, every single one of them, say I had talent, that I would go far? Yes, they did. Don't forget that, Connie. Hang on to that. And to this: They brought me books to read from their own libraries—the sweetest gifts.

But then something happened. Something horrible. What was it that went wrong?

.   .   .

I AM ASLEEP and I know this is only a nightmare, that I shouldn't take it seriously and that I should wake up. But I can't.

It is summer. Everything is green, the color of those apples Mama buys me at the store. I am four years old. I like being four—it means I will start kindergarten soon. I am playing in the backyard of our small house in Jacksonville Beach. I'm running through the heat on stubby legs when suddenly I stop. I see the snake sliding through thick blades of grass. It is black and red with golden eyes. Its pink forked tongue flickers, rising above the tips of the grass, searching me out. This snake is bad, evil even. I try to run to the house, but my legs turn to rubber. I cry and scream, but no one hears me.

Mama stands at the sliding glass doors smoking a cigarette, watching, not understanding the danger I'm in.

The phone rings. My heart beats rough and fast. I must wake up! I must rise up through these strange layers of sleep. The layers have colors—the deepest black to violet and finally indigo blue. I throw off the covers and feel my way into the kitchen. I must get there before the ringing stops. Hurry. Hurry. Katie is at my heels. I pray to God it's you. The prayer tastes rancid. No, that's not possible. Prayers do not have flavor. They are just words. Nothing more. I grab the phone.

"Hello, darling," you say in your radio voice.

"Where are you?"

"I'm working. Dancing on the moon. Doing my thing."

"But where are you?"

"If you must know," you say playfully, vowels booming, "I'm at a lady friend's house, and we're working on something big. Something for us, kid." You giggle insanely and my sleep-fogged mind suddenly snaps to, rushing from one hopeful possibility to the next. *Maybe Daddy is learning his lesson.*

"Are you there, Constance Anita May?"

"Yes, yes, I'm here."

"Of course you are. I need you to do me a favor, kid."

"Okay."

"Go see if my black trousers are clean and pressed and if not, get it done. ASAP. I've got to have them."

"All right. But why, what's happening?"

"Big things, my dear."

"Like what?" I'm trying to figure out the subtext, the order of life. "Where did you say you were?"

"Listen, other people need to use the phone. I've got to
go. See ya' later, kid. Don't stop dreaming about me."

"Wait! When are you coming home?"

You don't hear the question. You've already hung up.

Did I say something wrong? Did I sound understanding
enough? I didn't nag, did I? I retrace our conversation, keeping in mind that here you are, a man whose career is on
the ropes, a man who is trying to save himself. You are not
to blame for your indiscretions. You need a compassionate
woman. Someone who will stick with you through this bad
spell. Someone of infinite patience. A sweet woman. Mama
was forever yelling at Daddy. Maybe she drove him away.
Maybe he couldn't take her constant screaming. Right there
in my kitchen, where I have been known to huddle on the
floor as I recover from your blows, I promise myself—no, I
promise us—that I won't repeat Mama's mistakes. I will be a
good woman.

. . .

WITH KATIE IN TOW, I walk into the living room and dissect
all that I know: You need clean trousers.

I take this as a sure sign you will come home soon.

. . .

YOUR SUPERSONIC IBM Selectric typewriter is on the coffee table. That is where you keep it, as if by having it on display something miraculous will happen, like maybe a manuscript will appear.

I am not allowed to touch this typewriter. It's a very expensive machine. I might break it, you say.

But you are not here. And I cannot sleep.

Take a chance. Defy him.

There is a stack of paper, right there next to the typewriter. Clean and white and waiting for words. Just one sheet, a perfect piece of paper to write a poem on. That is all I need, all I dare pilfer. I look toward the door. Not a chance you'll walk in. You're out having a time. You will never know. My heart is racing. Sweat glistens like tears down my face. I insert the paper and type *M*. Then I sit there, frozen by fear and discouragement. Seconds stretch into minutes. Finally, I close my eyes and type *E*.

ME.

.   .   .

I DESTROY ALL EVIDENCE of my typewriter use. I make sure it is turned off and I straighten the ream of paper. I wipe off the keys. Then I take my poems into the kitchen and burn them in the sink.

.   .   .

IT'S A RAINY MORNING. I hope it storms all day. If it does, Bayshore will flood and Katie and I will walk down to the water and look at the rich people ensconced in their mansions. We will catch glimpses of them through their finely paned windows that shine like jewels. We will see them talking on phones to their insurance agents with the frantic boredom of the wealthy.

I get out of bed and pee. Katie follows me. She stands there, staring up at me, while I whiz. I pet her head and say goo-goo things to her. Then we return to the bedroom and Katie jumps onto the mattress, lies on her back, and squirms to and fro with her legs in the air. I don't know what she's doing. Maybe her spine is itchy.

The shirt I slept in stinks. I stink. I need to take a shower. But before I do, I stand in front of my vanity mirror and take stock. I turn my face from side to side. I have good cheekbones and clear skin, except for the freckles. Mama swore that some men liked freckles. I never believed her. Not then. Not now. I should splurge and buy a jar of that, what's it called? Porcelana? That stuff that is supposed to bleach away age spots, freckles, what have you. I widen my eyes and then flutter. My lashes are colorless, transparent. I'm one gene away from being an albino. *Check out lash dye.* In my mind I put a star by that sentence. I pull my strawberry blond hair into a tail at the nape of my neck. I imagine myself with slicked-back hair held tight with an unobtrusive length of ribbon. There I am, walking downtown in smart black pumps. Big gold earrings dangle from each lobe. I possess a sophisticated, don't-mess-with-me aura. A head turner, don't you know! Ha! The mirror doesn't lie, nor does it suffer fantasies. My ears stick out far too wide for me to ever pull off the slick sophisticate. My only saving grace regarding the ear problem is that my hair is so thick it covers them up. I move on to the bigger picture. I hold back my shoulders and suck in my gut. I have a good bustline, no one can take that away from me, but these days guys like flat-chested girls. Maybe I was born into the wrong era. Where's Jayne Mansfield and Sugar Doll when you need them? I turn sideways. Ugh! What I would give for a flat stomach! I continue my mental list, writing in a flourishing script: *Twenty sit-ups daily*. As for the ass, there's no hope. Nevertheless, I jot, *Tighten butt!* I turn forward and zero in again on my face. I try a smile à la *Mona Lisa*. Discreet. Superior. Serene. Not a tooth in sight. Then a larger smile, this time a flash of white but only for a second before the hand goes up. Don't reveal those teeth! Never, never, never! I curve my fingers and tilt my head. Feminine grace. Next, fingers together, hand flat, index finger on tip of nose, eyes rounded in surprise. Pert. Cute. Then your basic hand over mouth and chin. No—that looks too much like Mama trying to hide the fact of her missing teeth. Ah, shit. Who do I think I'm kidding? I let my hand drop. I flash a big, happy smile. And what I see shames me. It's what the world sees. It's what has prompted children and adults, alike, my entire life, to call me names. They have never hidden their cruelty. I suppose they think I am accustomed to the insults. That with a face like mine I deserve

them. Certainly anyone who looks like I do must be of diminished intelligence and therefore immune to the hurt
a normal person might suffer. Howdy Doody. Rabbit Face.
Monkey Face. Bucky. "Hey, you want a carrot, Rabbit Face!"
At that disco Debbie and Sue and I used to go to—what did
that guy say? "I hear girls with buckteeth give the best blow
jobs. So, whaddya think? We can go out to my van."

"Press on them!" That's what Mama ordered me to do.
"You don't need braces. Just put pressure on 'em."

Of course I needed braces. But we had no money, and I
have no money now. Mama's solution was better than not trying at all. When I was a kid, I would press so hard that my teeth
would ache and my fingers bleed. And it never did any good.

But now, on this rainy morning that offers the promise of
your return, I give Mama's cure one more try. With both
hands. I push as hard as I can. I grunt. And shake. The skin
around my mouth pales as my lips become blood engorged. I
think they might split open. But I don't care. I press even
harder. This is the best try yet. Tears start out of nowhere. I
hear myself scream. Katie suddenly sits up straight, on alert.
She jerks her head toward me, watching, raising her nose,
gaining the scent. She's got it, I can tell. Her nostrils flair
in and out as she consumes this secret smell. But does she
recognize it for what it is: self-loathing, untainted and unhinged? Does she know what I know: I am a creature so ugly
that you—a human more flawed than most—are the only man
willing to love me?

THREE DAYS LATER YOU RETURN.

No explanations are given, and I don't ask for any. I'm grateful to have you back. I must be doing something right. You didn't abandon me, after all. Not like Daddy did. Your black trousers are in the closet, pressed and cleaned, just like you asked.

You tell me you adore me. You tell me I'm precious. And then you give me a gift. A glass paperweight.

"It's gorgeous. Where did you get it?" I hold it to the light. Swirls of gold and blue rise like petrified smoke.

"I stole it!" you say triumphantly. "Right out of Steve's office."

"His law office?"

"Can you believe it! He turned his head once and— swipe!—the thing was in my pocket!"

I place the paperweight on the coffee table, uncertain of what to say. I don't want stolen goods.

"I thought you liked Steve."

"I love him!"

You settle onto the couch and light a cigarette. Katie comes over to greet you and you push her away.

"Listen, I've been talking to my guy out west. He thinks there's no reason I can't get a job up north. You know, a big market. Maybe Chicago. St. Louis. Kansas City. So I'm going to Iowa for a few weeks. I'll use his house as my base."

"Oh. Okay. You're going to drive all the way to Iowa?" Why are you leaving again? Are you going alone or with your latest fling? Are you really looking for a job or is this yet another lark? Wait, where is my positive nature? My caring, sacrificial, good-hearted nature? I must believe in your basic decency. You are a good man. You are trying to save yourself.

"No, I'm not driving. I'm flying." You snort and shake your head as if my driving comment is profoundly stupid.

You have no credit cards and no money, but you bought a plane ticket. I stare at the stolen paperweight, choking back my impulse to ask where the airfare came from. But I know better. Not asking is how I survive.

That afternoon when I get to work, I call the bank. Yes, a check made out to you cleared yesterday, they say. For two hundred and seventy-six dollars. My balance is twenty-three cents.

So, you forged my name again.

.   .   .

I DEAL WITH the forgery the way I deal with most everything else in my life: I make up reasons why your behavior is justified.

You need the money.

You don't see it as stealing since we are living together and I'm supporting you.

It is easier for you to simply take the money than to bother me with the mechanics of writing a check.

You are trying to rebuild your life. You are much worse off than I am. Complaining completely cancels out any points earned by possessing a giving heart.

Even if you had asked for the money, I would not have denied you.

You need my support.

You are all I have.

.   .   .

Two days after you leave, I step on the prong of a belt you left lying on the bedroom floor. It goes through the heel of my bare foot, a good two inches in. I pull it out and drive myself over to a clinic down the street where they give me a tetanus shot. Then I go to work.

.   .   .

Katie is frisky without you here. Maybe because there is no shouting. No ill will or violence.

In the fenced backyard she runs and digs holes and hunts mice. We play catch with an old tennis ball I found in a park. Sometimes she runs the perimeter of the yard, round and round, her ears pinned fast against her fur.

She's getting big and healthy. Her coat is shiny black

and her bones no longer appear to creak beneath a thin wafer of skin.

Every morning she wakes me by licking my face. She never stirs me when I'm in a deep sleep. She waits until I'm dreaming toward wakefulness.

How does she know I am approaching consciousness? Do my eyes dart behind my closed lids in this lighter stage of sleep? Do I give off a scent or a current?

Or does she?

What I'm getting at is this: Who is waking whom?

. . .

I HAVEN'T FELT WELL since the tetanus shot. At first it was just a little stomach queasiness but now, a week later, nothing stays inside me. Whatever I eat, out it goes. Even when I don't eat, my stomach is always working. Things issue out of me that, I swear, I never put in.

Katie stays by my side. To the bathroom, back to the bed, to the bathroom, back to the bed, never letting me out of her sight.

. . .

AFTER EIGHT DAYS, finally you call. You say you're making progress, that people remember you fondly, that they want a broadcaster of your caliber. "It's just a matter of time, baby," you say.

You offer no specifics and I don't push. "That's good," I respond. "I'm glad things are working out." But I can't muster much enthusiasm. I have, after all, heard it all before. And I don't feel well enough to feign optimism.

You demand to know what is wrong. You say you're out in the world busting your ass for us, and I don't even sound happy about it.

"I'm happy."

"Then act like it. A little support would be appreciated."

"I'm glad things are going well. I'm just . . . something is wrong. I think I'm sick."

"Don't start with me, you stupid bitch."

Your venom is quick. A sucker punch to the gut. I try to pinpoint my mistake but before I can, you hit again.

"The minute I leave you get sick. It's all in your head, kid. You are so fucked up. Well, you're not going to fuck me up this time, lady."

I hear a loud bang—I guess you are hitting a table or maybe a wall. *Stop, please stop!*

The line goes dead.

I stand in the kitchen, staring at the receiver, and I start to cry. I should never have made you mad. You are trying so hard. I dial the number. I will apologize. I will tell you how proud I am of you. I will beg your forgiveness. I let it ring twenty-two times. Finally I hang up, whispering, "No, no, no!" I try to slip into that white space—the place I sometimes run to inside myself when you are beating me, when Mama was beating me. Nothing lives there. I'm the only one allowed in. Pure white emptiness. Where the fuck is it? I cannot find it. My body is on fire—everything but my feet, and they are ice-block cold. Maybe the white space has been burned to a crisp. Or maybe it has locked me out. Maybe even the white space will no longer indulge me. I wander out of the kitchen, uncertain of what to do next.

"Katie!"

I hear the *thump* of her tail. She's lying on the floor beside the couch.

"Come on, Katie. Come with me."

My eyes ache. Acid tears. That's what I think as I wipe my nose on my sleeve and crawl into bed.

.　.　.

MY FRIEND JERRY, who is gay, lives in the upstairs apartment. We used to live together. It was a good arrangement. We gave each other advice about men all the time. It was fun. I had a beautiful bedroom up there, complete with a cream-colored carpet, a nice warm tone, and sapphire curtains. The afternoon sun filtered through the blue, casting everything in a golden hue. It was a peaceful, meditative place. I thought I might be able to pull my life together in a room like that.

But then you called and said you'd broken your knee and had no place to go (flat broke, that's what you said), and you asked if we would take you in. Just for a couple of months, you said.

Six months later, you were still there, mooching off us. My cream carpet turned gray under the pall of your cigarette ashes, and I could barely get to the door without stumbling over a wine bottle. I started referring to my room as the Wasteland. Still, I felt sorry for you. You were an old man whose star had passed, and you said you loved me. You kept making anguished promises about getting a job and turning me into someone I could be proud of.

But you with your many dependencies—smoke, drink, drugs—made a lousy roommate. Jerry couldn't stand living with you anymore, and I didn't blame him. But I couldn't get out. Each time I tried, you told me I was the only person in the world who cared about you. Without me, you couldn't go on. Maybe you would just kill yourself. Get it over with. Didn't I see how good we were together?

So I moved us into the apartment downstairs and waited for you to get well, or employed, or both.

.   .   .

JERRY AND I work together. He's a waiter and is studying mass communications and public relations at USF. He's very efficient. Clean-cut. Looks like the All-American boy. I bet he makes great tips. He doesn't know the whole story between you and me. He doesn't trust or like you, but the beatings and stuff are beyond him. He's not home very often.

.   .   .

BEING A BARTENDER at Bennigan's has its privileges. We're at the top of the employee pecking order. Even though we make our own tips, the wait staff is also required to tip us. We can make or break a waiter's night. Slow down their drinks or pour them weak, and the waiter has a disgruntled customer on his hands. So everybody is nice to us.

Slopping liquor isn't the half of it. We become our customers' confidants. They tell us shit they would never tell their wives or husbands. Lost jobs. Secret bank accounts. Illicit loves. Past lives. Fetishes. Sins. Dreams and lies. They are bored humans. Maybe they lack the intellect wonder requires.

I have a trick that wows them every time. I keep a highball glass filled with Cuervo Gold under the bar. When a customer reaches for a cigarette, I dip two fingers in the tequila, put a match to them, and offer the person a light with my flaming digits. It doesn't hurt. As soon as the liquor burns off, the flame goes out. But it sure is a crowd pleaser.

Some of my customers who are in their early twenties are already rock-hard alcoholics. They bruise my conscience much more than do the old drunks.

All of this sort of sickens me. I mean, between home and work, all I do is feed other people's addictions. Maybe that's my calling.

. . .

I HAVEN'T BEEN to work in a week. Seems like I'm either on the toilet or in bed, and sometimes I am delirious.

Katie jumps on the bed, which causes me to wince. My skin hurts. Even a sheet is too much. But I can't tell her to get down; that would hurt her feelings, and her intentions are too pure. She lies beside me, rests her head on my chest, and stares.

"It's okay, baby," I tell her, stroking her back. "I'm gonna be well soon."

My stomach makes a weird, sloshing, watery noise. It startles Katie. She sniffs my belly. She probably thinks I've got a rabbit in there.

I hear my front door creak open. Maybe it's you. Or maybe it's a rapist. I'm too sick to see anybody.

"Connie! It's Jerry."

"Oh, Jerry, come on in. I'm in the bedroom."

Katie jumps off the bed and runs to greet him. Jerry is very fit. He works out. Eats right. Has a killer smile and a tight, high butt. All the girls at Bennigan's want to convert him. Rita always says, "I wish he'd get over this gay thing."

He pets Katie, who has headed him off at the door. Then he looks up and seems startled by the sight of me.

"Gee, Connie, you look like hell. Why didn't you let me know you were this sick? I thought you just had the flu."

I tell him to bring over a chair. I tell him not to touch me.

.   .   .

FOR THE NEXT few days, Jerry is my nurse. He brings me broth and ginger ale.

I keep murmuring, "Thank you, thank you," and then I cry because I'm so grateful he's my friend.

He asks about you, and even though I put a really good spin on your absence (you're interviewing for some very important jobs in the Midwest—all very prestigious opportunities), Jerry looks past me and out my window and says, "What a creep."

.　.　.

I AM FALLING in and out of a feverish sleep. A phone is ringing. Jerry is saying, "Whatever is wrong with her is serious. You need to come home."

I yell, "Don't say anything else! Don't get me in trouble!" Or maybe I just think it. *Shut up, Jerrry. You'll make him mad.*

I know that this part really happens: Jerry comes into the bedroom with a glass of ice. He helps me sit up, and I cry out because it hurts to move or be touched. I take the ice and ask, "What did he say?"

My friend laughs and flashes that gorgeous smile and says gently, "He's an asshole."

.　.　.

THE NEXT MORNING, I'm too weak to get out of bed, so Jerry half-drags, half-carries me into the bathroom, sets me up on the toilet, helps me pull down my panties, and waits outside until I'm done.

"How are you doing in there?" he calls from just outside the door.

"Fine," and after a pause we both start laughing as the absurdity of my answer sinks in.

When I'm done, Jerry returns and helps me clean myself and pulls up my panties. I have no dignity left.

Once he gets me back into bed, he says, "We've got to call your sister."

"No! I don't want to bother her. She's got her hands full with the baby."

"Listen, Connie, I'm in charge now. Give me her number."

.   .   .

I TRY NEVER TO bother my brother or sister. They have their own troubles.

And just so you know, so you won't think I'm truly alone in the world with only you to lean on, when I talk about my brother and sister, I mean my mother's children. But I have other siblings. Daddy had two kids before he ever met Mama. We are not close but that doesn't mean we won't be one day. Bubba lives in St. Augustine and is probably twenty years my senior. I don't even know exactly. He's sort of like an acquaintance. Sissy lives somewhere up north. I've only met her once—at Daddy's funeral. I remember her as being really pretty. And nice. I'm telling you this so you'll understand that I have people. So maybe if I ever summon the courage to show up on their doorsteps, they might take me in.

Let me tell you about Mama's children.

Jimmy splits his time between Houston and Costa Rica and everywhere in between. I'm never sure where he's at. He moves around a lot. I think that by being in constant motion, he hopes to keep his ghosts at bay. Depression and self-doubt—those are his scorpion tails.

He knows more of the dirt about Mama and Daddy than any of us. His childhood was ravaged by their bad behavior. Their inability to put down roots resulted in his attending thirteen different public schools in a span of twelve years. He witnessed countless episodes of Daddy beating Mama. When he was old enough, maybe sixteen, he tried to put a stop to it. I'm not privy to the details, but I know fists were involved.

So I cannot tell Jimmy about the straits I'm in for many reasons. He's too far away. I'm scared of what he would do if he found out. I can't bare my shame to him. He would be so disappointed in me.

As for Deidre, she handles the burden of our childhood the way she always has—by allowing it to eat her alive. She gobbled down all of the abuse heaped on us, took every ounce of it in, and now there is no room for Deidre. She punishes the child she once was, the little girl Mama derided and beat, by refusing food. She weighs less than a hundred pounds. I've seen her convulsively cry, wracked with guilt and regret because she ate half of an apple.

I cannot add to her anguish.

But I also know I don't want to lie here and die. So I will let her know that I'm ill. But she will never know that you beat me.

. . .

DEIDRE IS GOOD and sweet. Without fuss, she takes me to the emergency room at Tampa General and stays with me until the wee hours of the morning.

. . .

I AM PROSTRATE on a gurney, an IV in my vein. Deidre paces, her face impassive, her shoulder bag clutched tight.

She is so thin, but still profoundly beautiful. We look nothing alike. Physically speaking, I am hopelessly Irish peasant: big boned, red hair, freckles. Deidre, on the other hand, looks as if she springs from noble stock. Ash-blond hair. Clear, lovely skin that tans. A feminine, delicate frame. Despite her problems, she has an air of grace. She was born with it.

. . .

TAMPA GENERAL IS a teaching hospital. Patients are seen by residents who have been awake for thirty hours and all have troubles and illnesses of their own.

The resident who sees me is in an ob-gyn rotation. Ovaries, Fallopian tubes, and cervixes consume him. They're all he thinks about. He takes my history and, without once actually looking me in the eye, says, "I suspect you're pregnant."

"That's not possible."

"Anything is possible," he snaps, returning his pen to his lab coat's breast pocket.

I try to explain why he's wrong, but he shakes his head as if he were a child refusing to hear his mother's truth. "Believe me, young women like you get pregnant all the time."

Ignoring the innuendo, I try again to explain.

"Look, he was walking across America when this golf ball comes out of nowhere and zaps him right in his . . ." I pause because I realize this story sounds insane and I begin to laugh uncontrollably, and the resident jots something down on my chart, and I'm pretty sure he's just ordered a psychological consultation.

. . .

"WELL, am I yet another victim of immaculate conception?" I quip when the resident returns to my gurney.

He ignores my joke, announces that I'm not pregnant, simply severely dehydrated. He seems depressed. In his world of "guess that disease," he just lost round one.

"It's okay," I tell him. "Maybe next time."

He nods morosely, orders intravenous fluids, chalks up

my condition to the flu, and sends me home with the admonition to drink more water.

· · ·

My body has turned on me. Nothing the doctors do, no off-the-shelf cure my sister brings to me, has any long-lasting effect. If I were one hair crazier, I'd think I was possessed. It's obvious I'm trapped in some sort of revolting cycle. My body tools along for about three days, emptying itself of all manner of alien life, and then I collapse because I'm dehydrated. It's always my sister who takes me to the emergency room.

· · ·

You're back in town, still broke and jobless, but too busy to care for me. You're the man of a thousand schemes. Movies. Commercials. Business enterprises. Scams. Your word, not mine.

As for my current condition, you continue to insist that I'm a psychosomatic maniac.

It's early morning, and I'm lying on the couch. I haven't slept in the bed since you returned home: your tossing and turning make my skin and muscles ache all the more. Katie stays on the floor, within my reach. I keep one hand resting on her shoulder. I'm running a fever. Deidre, who lives across town, is on her way over to check on me. You, of course, have something to do, but as always, the specifics elude us.

You loom over me, coffee cup in hand, and sigh as if I'm just far too much trouble.

"It's all in your head," you say, dismissive. "You want more attention from me. You want me all to yourself. But other people need me, too. I'm somebody in this town. I don't have time for your bullshit."

I start to cry. "It's not in my head, I swear to God!"

Right before you walk out the door, dressed to the nines in dry-cleaned clothes that I paid for, you say, "You're all on your own this time, kiddo."

.   .   .

I'VE BECOME A regular at the ER. If it weren't for the IV infusions, I'm convinced I would be dead.

But other than the IVs, this place is a joke. On average, I see three to four different residents per visit. They diagnose me according to their specialty. In the span of a single evening, I'm told I have inflammation of the brain, inflammation of the sac surrounding my heart, inflammation of my stomach lining, cancer (they don't say cancer of what), and an ectopic pregnancy. Then, as usual, they administer an IV and send me home.

.   .   .

Eventually, I grow so weak that the IV fluids don't help. The stumped doctors decide to admit me even though I'm uninsured. Before they wheel me from the ER to my room, a nurse takes my vitals, studies my chart, and then shoots me a decisive glance.

"Ah! You're an indigent," she says and then marches away in her bright white nurse's uniform.

. . .

I'm hospitalized for thirty days. In a quad. I'm naturally curious, so initially I try to get to know my roommates.

The woman in the bed across from mine is in her mid-thirties and is in love with her gall bladder surgeon. When her husband isn't around, she wails her surgeon's name as if she's a lovesick teenager, and then we both giggle hysterically.

Postsurgery, in the middle of the night, the nurses descend and order her to "move her bowels."

She tries. She sits on the bedpan and screams.

An old diabetic black woman is assigned to the bed on my left (I've got the window that affords me a great view of the boiler room). She's on kidney dialysis and spends on average about a week a month in the hospital. It's not so bad, she says, because the food is good. She has large numbers of visitors: sons, daughters, nieces, nephews, cousins, the whole shebang.

My other roomy is an old white woman who is very sick, but I don't know of what. The nurses won't tell me. She has blue translucent skin. None of us know her name. Apparently, she hasn't any family. She dies while we watch.

Both Gall Bladder and Diabetic (names, I learn, become far less memorable than the illnesses that afflict us) are discharged my first week here. New patients come and go so quickly, usually when I'm asleep or out for tests, that I stop keeping track. There's no need to talk or make temporary friends. We're dehumanized in this place. We are charts and lab tests and bedpans. We are not whole. We are not precious, unique individuals. We are our disease.

. . .

YOU COME TO SEE ME twice for about three minutes, total. You are busy. You are working on something big, you say.

For once I'd like to hear you say, "I'm working on something small, something of no consequence whatsoever."

But I keep that wish to myself.

. . .

I'M WORRIED ABOUT KATIE. You refuse to take care of her. You say you are too busy. So she lives outside, mainly. My sister checks on her. Makes sure she has water and food, as does Jerry. They assure me she is doing fine. I ask one of the nurses if there is any way I can get permission for my dog to visit. She stops fiddling with my sheet, looks up at me, and laughs.

. . .

EVERY DAY THE DOCTORS run tests, and every day they come up stumped.

They decide to perform an endoscopy. A cordial East Indian doctor whose surname is composed almost entirely of vowels explains, smiling, that they are going to run a tube up my butt. He says, full of excited wonder, that the end of the tube has a camera on it, and that they are going to take pictures of my intestinal tract.

"Will it hurt?"

"Not really. You'll be sedated."

Then he has me sign a release form that states modern medicine is not an exact science, so that I shouldn't take any of this too seriously—death, life, whatever—we're all just muddling along and—hey!—mistakes happen.

The nurse brings in a second form. It is, in essence, a model's release. It explains that the hospital can take pictures of my butt and inner workings (as many as the doctors deem necessary) and that the photographs can be reproduced in textbooks from here to eternity without me giving any further permission.

I'm confused. I seek clarification. "So the hospital will

own images of my behind? And can do anything with them they want?"

"Essentially."

. . .

I'M GRATEFUL that weeks ago I lost my dignity. Seems that since this is a teaching hospital and I'm a bit of a mystery patient, the operating theater is packed. I'm lying on the gurney (they haven't yet given me a sedative), and I watch as the viewing area fills up with young, curious, handsome, primarily male faces. And I realize that I know some of them. These guys drink at Bennigan's. Happy hour regulars. I start to panic. I can't do this. A nurse tells me to calm down, that everything will be okay. She orders me to lie on my side. She fusses with the sheet, fully exposing my big white butt.

Then she gives me a shot, and within seconds the smiling, familiar faces go blurry.

. . .

FINALLY, after a full month, the doctors figure out the obvious. I have salmonella, one of the worst cases they've ever seen.

At the foot of my bed, the doctors discuss my illness among themselves, as if I'm not present.

"Don't know why we didn't check earlier."

"Wonder where she got it? Maybe it has something to do with the tetanus shot."

"Doesn't really matter. It's not like there's an epidemic or anything."

"Well . . . there's nothing we can do."

"Yep. It's just got to run its course."

.   .   .

I AM RELEASED without pomp or circumstance.

A nurse comes in to take the blood pressure of a new patient whom I've dubbed Heart Palpitation. Right before she pumps up the cuff, she looks over her shoulder and says, "Oh, honey, you can go home now."

I call the house for you to come get me, but there's no answer. I try my sister. I let the phone ring ten times before I realize she probably unplugged it so that her baby could get an uninterrupted nap. And Jerry is at work. So I bundle my few belongings (toothbrush, pajamas, the jeans and tee I wore the night they admitted me), and I walk home in clothes my sister brought me days earlier. The walk takes about a half hour and I sort of enjoy it. The fresh air—nothing antiseptic or putrid.

.   .   .

KATIE IS WAITING for me at the back fence. She jumps so high, she nearly clears the gate. She leaps into my arms. She has grown and smells of earth. Little dog tears track down her face.

"I'm sorry," I say. "Mama didn't mean to leave you. I missed you so much!"

She then leads me on a tour of her handiwork: a series of tunnels spanning the entire backyard. She has created an underground labyrinth, a cave system where no one can get to her. It must be cool in there, and so, so safe.

"Good girl. You are such a smart girl!"

She is proud of her accomplishment. I can see that in the way she prances.

I take her by the collar, lead her through the gate, and up to the porch. It's only then that I notice the piece of paper nailed to the screen door. Probably a flyer. Probably somebody trying to sell me something. No, no, this looks too official. Katie jumps up and places her front paws on my belly. With one hand I rub her shoulders and with the other I follow the crisply typed words pounded out by a bureaucrat in some cubbyhole downtown.

We have thirty days to vacate the property. By notice of the sheriff.

"Get down, Katie."

I remove the eviction notice from the door's pine frame. I hold it carefully, wanting nothing more than to wad it up and throw it away—in someone else's garbage, of course. *Please, God, I hope my neighbors didn't see this.* But I do not tear it up or otherwise harm it, for fear I'd be arrested for destroying government property.

I bring Katie inside and fix her a bowl of food and me a cup of tea. I've never been evicted before, so I really don't know what to do. I reread the notice five times, looking for clues on how to behave.

. . .

I DON'T FOOL AROUND. I've been out of the hospital for less than twenty-four hours, and I'm back at work, trying to be positive, trying not to dwell on the truth: There is no way I can raise enough money in thirty days to get us into a new place. I'm drowning in medical bills. Drowning in utility bills, your car payment, and sundry other charges you didn't pay while I was sick.

After my shift, at three o'clock in the morning, as you sit in your underwear watching an old movie and drinking wine, I try to explain this to you. I even go so far as to point out that our phone service is in danger of being disconnected and our electricity, no doubt, will be next. You simply call me a bitch and tell me to fix it.

"You knew about the eviction notice, and you didn't do anything. You didn't even take it off the door."

You close your eyes and take a huge gulp of wine. Then you return your gaze to the gray tones flickering on the tube.

"That's because," you say, calmly, your condescension forming every word, "it's not my problem."

. . .

I REFUSE TO ASK my sister for money. She has a baby and her husband works days as a teacher and nights as a horn player in a band. They are barely making ends meet.

If I were back in school in Drama 101 and my life was a play, Professor Luter would ask, "What is your motivation?" and this time I would know.

This time, without hesitation, I would say, "Shame."

.   .   .

KATIE IS ASLEEP on the floor on my side of the bed. You lie in a slumberous heap, on your side, snoring. I am staring at the ceiling, plotting a new life. In the morning, I will look for another job. One that's better paying, one that's more professional, one that suits my skills and education. *I can do it, I can do it, I can do it.*

This is my mantra, anemic and unpoetic.

.   .   .

HOW DO I explain the sudden knowledge that I cannot breathe?

From a deep sleep I awake to my own body convulsing as it struggles for air. The body never gives up without a fight. No, it doesn't. Even though the lack of oxygen is causing my fledgling perceptions to flake and scatter, I absolutely know something horrific is happening. Nightmarish details bloom from these breathless shadows. For instance, I know that an enormous weight is crushing my neck.

I try to move—I must flee from this situation—but I cannot. A body far larger than mine pins me to the mattress. In my fight to free myself, I manage to gain control of one arm. With it, I flail and hit.

My attacker is grunting, bringing all his weight to bear on my throat. What is he using? Not his hands. As I struggle in the dark, trying to figure out what is happening and how to save myself, the headlights of a passing car momentarily illuminate the room.

You are killing me. I see the outline of your mouth, how your lips are stretched into two thin lines as they curl back against your gritted teeth. For one brief moment I glance into your eyes. They are small and lightless, as if for you murder carries no emotional baggage. Perhaps you are not truly awake. Maybe you are trapped in a nightmarish state. Like a zombie or the living dead. You are pressing your forearm into my throat. You are bringing all of your weight to bear. Your breath pulses against my face in short, violent bursts.

I am terrified, which is a good thing. Terror outpaces pain. The room goes black once more. I feel tendons and tissue and muscle and tiny bones begin to give. Try to grab a breath. No. There is no room in my windpipe. Not even an invisible wafer of air can slip through. Breathe through the nose. That should keep me going. No. Doesn't help. Can't reach my lungs.

But the smell. The stench of liquor, cigarettes, sweat. Alcoholics smell funny, as if their pores ooze poison. Why are you killing me?

I try to yell for help or plead with you to stop, but you have immobilized my vocal chords. I fear that my larynx is about to break open. In my mind's eye, I watch as you turn my voice box into a bloodied rose, smashing its tiny muscle mass with steady, intense weight. I hear myself make gurgling, sinus-afflicted noises. It's not anything I can control. The sounds emit not from my throat, but from somewhere else. Maybe my nose? Maybe inside my head? Or chest? Who knows, who knows, who can help me?

You switch from your forearm to your hands. You continue to press hard with your palms as your fingers curl and squeeze.

It is a liquid darkness that ferries me toward unconsciousness. Split-second sensations, involuntary recognitions bleed loosely into one another. What is touch? Taste? Sight? Sound? They are all one. A single ripple forever flowing in a river so fearsome I cannot speak its name. Time does not exist in this place of silver fish and mud. It is neither slow nor fast. There is no clock ticking away. No absolute measuring stick marking the distance between one world and the next. This is the resurrection place, where the distinction between the living and dead blurs.

Despite the fact that I am near death—that you are murdering me—my primal survival instinct is intact, if only by that single sheaf of air sipped on by a hungry lung. How else can I explain the sudden wisdom—the swift, jarring wherewithal—to push myself back, back, back, as far into the waterbed mattress as I possibly can?

At this moment, as your destruction of me gains momentum, as I float deeper into the drowning pool, I know only one thing: If I create a little room—just a hair's width—I buy what doesn't exist. Time.

. . .

I GIVE UP. This is it. I'm near the bottom. But the bottom has an opening. Small and bright. Like a metal shard flashing under a hard sun. I do not know where it will lead. Perhaps to more dying. Maybe this is the continued fulfillment of the curse, that I shall die eternally. I cannot believe this is happening. Pain and terror have morphed into shocked disbelief. I am not suppose to die like this. I simply don't believe it's time for me to go.

My arrogance is astonishing, the arrogance of the living to try to refuse death. Face it: I am almost dead. Allow the water in. It is the water that will dissolve my will, my youthful human arrogance.

Let it come.

. . .

DID GOD DO THIS? Did he force you into behaving with all the whimsy of a precocious, spoiled child? Was it divine intervention that made you stop? Without explanation? Without apology? Without apparent remorse or anger? Or maybe it was Mary, the Mother of God, who made you sit up, rub your hand over your face, roll over, and go back to sleep.

Then again, maybe it was shit dumb luck.

. . .

KATIE JUMPS ONTO the bed and lies between us.

Scared to move, I lie rigid, watching the window, praying for daylight, knowing only one thing: I will never understand what just happened.

Evil, I think, *you are solely and profoundly evil.*

. . .

I LIE MOTIONLESS, trapped in darkness so resolute that even shadows cannot penetrate.

. . .

THE FEAR IS you have inflicted permanent damage.

The fear is you have battered my larynx and vocal chords into pulp.

The fear is you will rise up again and finish the job.

The fear is if I move a muscle in order to flee, you will do more than strangle me.

The fear is if I stay in this room, paralyzed by your violence, you win.

.   .   .

I move quickly. Silently. I pretend to possess the omni-
scient quality of air. I cannot see the door. I am not sure
when to make the small left turn that will lead me out of here.
So I rely on my dog. I follow the soft sound of her paw pads on
the wood floor.

.   .   .

Our instincts are in sync. Katie and I head for the kitchen.
There I lock the door. I pour cream into a pan and slightly
warm it. I set it on the floor. She laps it, pausing once to look
up at me. I know I would be dead without her. Somehow, she
keeps me safe.

I break ice cubes out of their plastic tray, wrap them in a
damp dishcloth, and apply this cold compress to my throat.

I wish there was a chair in this kitchen. An upholstered
cushy job that when I sat in it I felt swallowed up. I pour tap
water into a plastic cup and ease onto the floor, my back
against the doors that hide the sink's plumbing. Katie lies
beside me and rests her head in my lap. I rub her ears. It
hurts when I move my head.

"We have to figure things out, Miss Katie," I say, wincing,

shocked by how painful it is to speak, surprised by the thin rasp of my voice.

Maybe I should go to the emergency room. Maybe I'm hurt bad. Maybe I'm bleeding internally and my belly will fill with blood and I'll die. No, no. No more medical bills. No more doctors. No prodding questions that might lead me toward speaking the shameful truth. How would I explain my injuries? Those nurses are smart. They'll never believe me. No, wait! I've got it! An intruder. He gained entry through an open window. I played dead. He stopped once he thought he had killed me.

. . .

I CANNOT GO TO the hospital. I cannot leave Katie alone with you. I cannot face friends or strangers.

. . .

ON TIPTOE, I sneak into the living room, grab the cushions off the couch, and take them with me into the kitchen.

. . .

IT'S MUCH MORE comfortable in here now. The floor was hard. I feel like I'm three years old playacting like I'm an adult. Only there aren't any games to play. There is time and there are questions. That's it. So I sit here, Katie by my side, staring into space, waiting for daybreak. I am drinking cheap wine. It hurts to swallow, but that's a price I'm willing to pay in order to try to feel better about this night.

I am in a morbid mood. The wine, I decide, is the color of blood. My blood. Mama's blood. My sister's, too.

How can I make sense of the harm you have done me without conjuring memories past, without placing the ugly details in the palm of my hand and inspecting them bit by bit, searching for answers as if I were an oracle reading dust?

. . .

HERE IS MAMA'S LIFE:

She was an angry woman who believed life had let her down.

And it had.

She was born in the Appalachian village of Grundy, Virginia, the first child of George and Rose Looney, descendants all of Belfast, dyed-in-the-wool Roman Catholics, and poorer than the dirt on which their shack sat.

All I know of these people I gleaned from the stories my mother spun.

Rose Looney was a gentle, loving mother. I carry her picture around with me to this day. It is the only photograph I have of any of my grandparents. Uncle Marshall, according to family lore, was a decent man, a productive soul, and a state senator. Grandma Looney drank 'shine, smoked a pipe, played the Autoharp, and lived to nearly a hundred.

That's all I know about the good side. The evil part comes now.

Mama's father was not a kind man. She claimed he displayed the worst attributes of the Irish. He was a hard drinker with a wicked temper. But does being Irish explain why he routinely beat his wife and child, and why he contracted syphilis and infected his wife?

Rose died while giving birth to a stillborn baby. In the aftermath of Rose's death, George and Mama moved to Richmond. There, one night while waiting for a bus, she was raped by three men. Not her father, nor her Irish temper, nor her humble Appalachian upbringing could explain why that terror was inflicted on her.

She ran away from home, and perhaps in an effort to appease an intolerant God who had proffered her no favors, she joined a convent. She claimed she had taken all but her final vows when the good priest told her she exuded far too much life to spend hers behind the veil.

Mama had her talents. For instance, she possessed perfect pitch. In fact, before I came along and before his stint as a cop, Daddy had his own country and western band. Mama was his coach and manager.

She wasn't an uneducated woman. She'd taken college-level courses in English, journalism, nursing. While in Washington, D.C., she heard Pablo Neruda (in the flesh) read his poems. Her taste in music was eclectic and smart: Tchaikovsky to Monk to Williams to Cream. She could discuss history and art and politics. She could paint and sew and knit and cook. She was liberal and bullheaded and intellectually curious.

She was, in short, a woman of ascending potential.

I do not know the moment of her downfall. I suspect it did not occur in a stunning, single crash of cymbals, but unfolded slowly, a dirge hauntingly played out through the generations, its origins across the sea in poverty-swept Ulster.

Or maybe, like me, she was cursed.

Cling to this fact: She was the mother of three children (one by a previous marriage, a son twelve years my senior), and she fought for us to have a better life than hers.

Nothing Daddy did diminished her love for him. Not her busted nose. Or her knocked-out teeth. Or the endless parade of other women he subjected her to. Booze and guns and fisticuff brawls—this was the world we lived in. Yet she fought like a wildcat to hang on to him, to make him into the man she dreamed he could be.

When he died at fifty years of age, her work wasn't finished; he still wasn't the family man she envisioned. And what's worse, her happiness died with him.

Maybe her quest to transform wayward men began back in Grundy when, as a small girl, she tried to please her daddy, even as she prayed for his transfiguration. And maybe, when she first laid eyes on Henry May, she recognized in his wild flame of a gaze her own father. And perhaps, even in the midst of tears and broken bones, she wasn't trying to save the man she married as much as she was trying to remodel, recreate, make better the man who sired her.

Daddy didn't know he was repeating George Looney's sins. And Mama never saw that she was attempting the horribly romantic but impossible feat of salvaging two lost souls (one from whom she'd fled) simply through the steadfast fierceness of her sacrificial love.

When Daddy died, he left behind the same person George Looney had created: a physically and spiritually fractured woman. With two girls to raise all by herself and not a clue how to manage, she plunged deeper into the family tradition: mean bitterness fueled by liquor.

She constantly railed at Deidre and me (and before he left home, my half brother Jimmy) in an effort, she said, to make us better people. She told us that we were worthless, that we were so incorrigible no one else would ever love us.

We were, she screamed, fat whores. We made her life miserable. We were all she had. She hated us. She loved us. We were angels or devils. Sluts or saints. There were no gray tones in our house. Only the extremes of the wretched.

Even though I was only seven when Daddy died, she was fond of saying I caused his death. "He couldn't stand your bad ways. He couldn't take you anymore. You're the reason he's dead. You killed Henry May!"

While I was so evil I killed Daddy, Deidre, who is six years older than me, was simply a burden.

"With God as my witness, I have no idea where you came from. You are so goddamn stupid."

As mean as Mama's mouth was, she was even better with her hands. She could slap us out of nowhere, or slam a coffee cup into the sides of our heads, or even throw a fisted punch, and we never, ever saw it coming. My sister and half brother and I have been whipped with hands, hoses, pots, pans, switches, shoes, belts, brushes, boards, brooms. We know about bruises and how to cover them up. We're good at it. Masters of disguise, physical and otherwise.

Why do I feel a faint stir of pride about this? Knowing how to hide bruises. Being facile at devising excuses for missing work and school. Fooling my schoolmates, teachers, and coworkers into believing I have a lovely home life. I should not be proud of these abilities. I should not view myself, for instance, as talented. But I do.

Yes, here I am, hiding in my kitchen, huddling on the floor, valuing my ability to survive, gauging what danger I will be in if I leave, understanding that I am my mother's daughter. And that she taught me well.

.   .   .

Dawn announces itself as a whisper of light.

It is the light I need. In the light I find the courage to lift myself off the floor and leave this bunker of a kitchen.

In the light, I decide, last night will become memory. And memories can be buried. Forgotten. In the light, life can go on as though the night never happened.

With Katie at my heels, I peek into the bedroom. You are snoring loudly. Your left arm is flung to my side of the bed, and your right forearm covers your eyes.

How do you sleep so comfortably? Are you incapable of experiencing guilt or remorse? Maybe you are king of the buried memory.

I ease away from the door, not turning my back on you until I am well beyond striking range.

. . .

KATIE FOLLOWS ME into the bathroom. She wags her tail, licks my leg, and then lies in front of the shower. The tile is cool and probably comforting.

I stand before the mirror and inspect the damage. My throat—now a testament to your violence—is banded in purple and blue and black. I gingerly touch the bruises. They are exotic. Celestial, even. I am sickened by the fact that I find my damaged flesh fascinating. I say to myself, "What have I learned?" Gaze at the girl in the mirror—that unwilling oracle whose neck is orbited by the rings of Saturn—and ask her, "What does the dust say?"

There are no hesitant predictions here. To my surprise, this prophecy, this divination conjured from an ashen past, is not born of dust at all. Rather, it is a sad old truth forged from crystal and fire and bone. It is an objective truth, unclouded by pity or fear. It offers no long-term hope. It is, in both scope and intent, insanely practical.

And I want to share it with you. I want to run into the bedroom and wake you up and shout in your face the only

thing I know, hoping the words and my stubborn resilience
will hurt you.

Here is the prediction, what the damaged girl in the mirror whispers. It is what I want to shout: Now that you have
strangled me, getting rid of the evidence through the deft use
of foundation and loose pink powder will be a breeze.

.   .   .

Two days later, with a scarf tied jauntily at my neck, I load
Katie into my Torino and take her to a vet in Clearwater. It's a
long drive in tough traffic, but I hear this guy is the best vet in
the area. I don't want her to bear any babies. I don't want her
to ever go into heat. I don't want her ever to be fucked.

After I sign Katie in, they take her into the back and then
hustle me into a darkened room where I am required to watch
a video about responsible dog ownership.

.   .   .

You profess no responsibility for strangling me. You
say it never happened.

I am incredulous at your denials. I must force you to admit what you did. I need a confession even more than I need
an apology.

In a voice made thin and weak from the attack, I ask,
"Then how do you explain the bruises?"

"For all I know, you did it to yourself, you crazy bitch."

In my through-the-looking-glass condition, I wonder if you're right.

.   .   .

IN THREE WEEKS a sheriff will come to our apartment, drag all of our belongings into the yard, and padlock the door.

I try to explain this to you. I suggest you help us find a solution.

"If you want a new apartment so bad, then find the money," you yell.

"We're being evicted. It's not about wants. We have no choice."

"Fuck you," you say, and then you get in your shiny silver Audi and head out.

.   .   .

THIS IS THE abandonment dance: Each time you run away, my father looms.

.   .   .

MY DADDY WAS good to me. That's what makes him being dead so awful.

Even though when it happened I was just a little kid and now I'm going on nine, I remember all them things that happened that night. For some reason I can't forget. Not like Mama. When she's drinking and smoking, she says to me, "Child, I don't ever want to hear your father's name spoken in this house. Do you understand me?"

"Why, Mama?"

" 'Cause I can't take the goddamn memories. That's why!"

So I keep 'em to myself. I don't talk to her about how the three of us, Mama, Deedee, and me piled into the car, leaving the fried fish to go cold on the stove. Or how pretty the night was, so full of stars I decided that maybe one day I could be an astronaut. Or how that black cat crossed in front of us, right to left, on Penman Boulevard, and how we all shivered at the sight of it. Or how happy Daddy was at that bar in Atlantic Beach. How he stood in the parking lot, threw back his head, and breathed so deep I thought he'd suck the stars right out of the sky, and then how he started laughing right out of nowhere.

I don't tell her this either: That night after we came home, Daddy lay on the couch watching TV, and he let me jump and crawl all over him. I bet I was irritating him, climbing on him like he was my own private mountain. But he didn't say one nasty word. That's how nice he was.

It was past my bedtime. I wasn't hardly ever allowed to stay up late enough to watch Johnny Carson. But I did that night.

Daddy was laughing, enjoying the show. Then that big guy named Ed started talking about how beautiful the talented

Angie Dickinson was. I wonder if he really meant it, or if he was just saying it 'cause Angie was their guest.

Anyway, Johnny told the audience to give Angie a warm welcome. They did. They clapped like all get-out.

She stepped out from behind that curtain, waving her beauty-queen wave and walked the length of the stage without tripping even once. I think she was what they call a blond bombshell. High heels. Teased hair. And a skintight sequin number—not at all ladylike.

Maybe that's why Daddy decided it was time for me to go to bed. He said, "Give me some sweet sugar, sunshine."

And I did. I kissed him good night.

Then I went to the bathroom and peed, washed my face, soaped up my hands, and daydreamed for maybe two minutes about being grown up and beautiful and maybe even a sexpot. I wiped off on the pink towel with the white seashells, and then I went on down to my room.

Mama and Deedee was in there, lying in our bed talking about boys and giggling to beat the band. I got under the covers. I was gonna try to sleep. We had to get up early. It was a school night. I don't know why Mama and Deedee were acting the fools. Usually Mama was tough on us.

I even finally said, "Y'all need to go to sleep!"

And they laughed like that was the funniest thing they'd ever heard. They were misbehaving like I couldn't believe. It was as if they was girlfriends having a slumber party.

Maybe that's why what happened next will never leave me, the good and the bad—bang, bang, bang—happening just like that.

I was tossing and turning, trying to get comfortable, and Deedee was talking about this boy she had a crush on, a boy named Buzzy (isn't that a funny name!),when all of a sudden a horrible noise shut her right up. Something pounded on the wall in the hallway. And then I heard that pretty picture of seagulls flying over the ocean waves, the one that Mama bought at Woolworth's, crash to the floor. And then somebody started making monster sounds. How did a monster get into the house? Where was Daddy? What was he doing? Was he okay? Had the monster killed him? The noise got louder and closer. The monster was coming down the hall. He was gonna get us, I just knew it!

"Oh my God, Henry, no!"

That's what Mama said right before she ran out of the room. No, "Sleep tight, don't let the bedbugs bite," or nothing. Only, "Oh my God, Henry, no!"

And then I knew. Daddy was the monster. Mama had always called him that. I'd heard her scream at him when they was fighting, "You're a monster!"

And now it had come true.

He didn't love us no more. He was mad at us. And hateful.

Did I do something wrong? Had I made him stop loving me? How come Daddy didn't love me no more?

I started crying. We were going to be torn to pieces. He'd eat us, pick his teeth with our bones. Must be 'cause I was so bad, like maybe I told a lie. Lies can cancel out love. That's what Mama always said.

We had to hide.

"Deedee, go close the door," I whispered.

And even though she usually wouldn't do anything I said, 'cause I was the little sister and she didn't like me bossing her around, this time she did. She leapt off the bed and shut the door and then spun back around, took me by both arms, pulled me off the bed, and shoved me into the tiny space between the mattress and wall.

Together we huddled there, praying out loud. "Dear God, don't let anything bad happen to us. . . . We'll be better daughters. . . . Don't let Daddy stop loving us. . . ."

I don't know how long we stayed like that—whimpering, crying, praying, saying out loud we were going to die, 'cause if we spoke the words then for sure they wouldn't come true. It seemed like we were there for hours, but maybe we really weren't—you know, time slows down when bad stuff is happening. I started rocking back and forth and whispering my daddy's name—"Daddy, Daddy, Daddy"—when suddenly the racket stopped, every single stitch of it.

It was so quiet that if I hadn't been hysterical scared I could have probably heard the stars moving in the wind. And even though things had quieted down, Deedee and me stayed as still as we could, trying not to even blink.

Don't know what she was thinking. As for me, I figured

the monster had killed Mama and we were next. *Come back, Daddy, don't let the monster stay. . . .*

I whispered, "What are we gonna do?"

"I don't know."

So there we sat in pitch darkness, waiting to meet our fate, wondering if Daddy was ever gonna come back to his senses. In my head, I damned the black cat who had crossed our paths.

I hugged my sister tight and closed my eyes. The bedroom was darker than the night behind my eyelids. *Daddy won't kill me. He won't. He won't. Daddy won't kill me. He won't. He won't.*

Somebody was wailing. It was real soft at first, sort of like the music you might hear in a dream. Then it grew louder and louder and louder. As the noise filled my ears I realized this wasn't no dream. Mama was crying.

What were us kids to do? Maybe she had killed the monster. Maybe it attacked her and she killed it dead. She saved us. But if she killed the monster, was Daddy dead, too?

I was scared beyond belief and pretty confused, but I told myself, *That don't matter, grow up! We have to go to her, have to smooth her hair off her forehead, have to find her cigarettes since she probably can't find them for herself.*

So Deedee and me, pretending we was brave, we stood up. Skin to skin, we left that room and wandered down the hall, and there was Mama on her bed, crying over Daddy's still body.

He was dead. Daddy was dead. It was a bad heart attack.

No chance of living. Even now, when I'm almost nine years old, the words don't comfort me. They cut me to pieces. Bits and pieces.

He ain't never gonna love me again.

.   .   .

ACCORDING TO THE smooth-voiced disc jockey on the classical music station, it is ninety-five degrees, and it's not yet noon.

I gaze at my reflection in the bedroom mirror and readjust the folds of my green turtleneck so that not one hint of my makeup smeared bruises show.

In twenty minutes I'll be in my Torino, heading across the bay for a job interview. A small, family-run newspaper needs an editor. Published monthly, the paper covers issues affecting the local personal computing scene. I know nothing about computers but my resumé regarding publishing is impressive for a recent college grad. High school and university newspapers, lots of honors, and not so much experience that they can't afford me.

That's what I tell myself. And also, *Breathe deeply*.

.   .   .

THERE ARE SO MANY things I don't say.

I don't mention you, for instance, even though you being recently famous might help my cause.

If I said something to the effect that we worked together on a few projects, they would most likely be impressed. After all, didn't they just see you in a commercial on TV? They would try to behave disinterested even as they quibbled over what exactly you were pitching. And it wouldn't cross their minds that the ad was shot three years ago. They would never suspect that you're penniless and mooching off me.

But no, I've got a chance here at a real job, I don't want to risk blowing it by spinning you.

But there is more.

The southern accent? I consciously can it by shortening my vowels, suspecting as I do that this quartet of interviewers are northern transplants who might mistake a drawl as a sign of a slow mind.

My buckteeth? I smile only with my lips clamped shut. I can't do anything about my overbite profile. So I try to draw attention away from my mouth by using a soft-colored lipstick but bold eye makeup.

Eviction notice?

Near death by strangulation?

A neck so spectacularly bruised that if I were to show it to them they would boomerang from shock, to concern, to revulsion?

Not a word. Not a peep. Not a single tremulous syllable.

Yes, I stick with my skeleton of a resumé, resolutely refusing the opulent flesh of both my distant and recent pasts which are, of course, the core of me. *White trash, ugly slut, fat bitch, dumb ass, hate you hate you hate you, you stupid cunt* . . . These words live inside me, always, pulsing to the cha-cha of my heartbeat. The song doesn't change just because I'm in the middle of a job interview. It's the volume that must be fiddled with. I can't operate in the world with the past blaring full blast. So even as I prattle on about my college experience, I work hard at turning who I truly am into background noise. Muzak of the damned. I believe I'm succeeding. I hear myself say, "I think you could improve the circulation of the newspaper by making just a few changes in the content and appearance of the various . . ."

.   .   .

I STEP ONTO the porch. You have dragged your "strictly off-limits" IBM Selectric outside. You have set it on a wobbly aluminum side table next to the front door. A small stack of typed pages lie beside your feet, kept in place by a nearly empty bottle of Gallo chablis wine.

"Hey, kiddo, how'd it go?" you ask.

"I think pretty well. They have some other people to interview. They said they'd let me know in a couple of days."

You begin to tell me about "our project," referring to the freshly typed wine-stained pages. "Hollywood is gonna love this. We're talking major motion picture!"

Katie scratches at the door. You continue to talk about "our" brilliant screenplay as I let her out. She jumps on me and smiles. It's a huge grin—the largest doggie smile, I'd bet, on the planet. Her lips curl up and back, revealing a mouthful of impressive canine pearly whites.

"What a gorgeous smile!" I coo at her, and the tension fostered by the job interview begins to ease off.

"You're not listening to me."

"Yes, I am."

"Then leave the fucking dog alone."

I stop petting Katie. "Sit!" I tell her, trying not to sound too stern. I press my leg against her so she'll know I wasn't scolding.

"So," I say, trying to give you my rapt attention, "you've been working."

"Goddamn straight!" you say, your eyes lit brightly from booze. "Oh, baby, I think we've really got something. Here, read the pages."

You pull them out from under the bottle, which tumbles over and rolls off the porch, clinking against the concrete step.

"I want your honest opinion."

"What do you mean?"

"I mean, help me write it. Get in there and fix things. This is *our* script. We're in this together."

"Really?"

You rub your hand across your mouth. Your eyes tear up.

"Absolutely. This could be it for us, kiddo. We might even make enough to get your teeth fixed if we play it right."

Fuck you. Eat dirt.

"I don't want you to hold anything back, you understand?"

I nod yes. My feelings get hurt too easily. Here you are, trying to help me and my response to your teeth comment is to secretly curse you. I should be more grateful.

You step off the porch, raise your arms to shoulder level and spin once. "Weeee!" You look wildly happy, as if you've just won the Nobel prize or a million bucks. "This is it, kiddo! I really mean it. Don't let me down!"

"Where are you going?"

"Round the corner."

You head to your car, and I know that when you return you'll be completely blasted. Right before you slip into the beautiful silver skin of your Audi, you say, "Write on the pages. Don't touch the typewriter. Now get to work."

I wave good-bye. You speed away. I kneel down and rub Katie's ears. She licks my cheek.

"Who knows, Katie? Maybe he's right." I hold on tight to my dog, trying to believe in your wisdom.

. . .

THERE WAS A TIME when I never doubted you. Even before I met you, I believed you possessed both the humanity and brilliance to save me. I've told you this before, but you always pretend not to be listening: I was eleven years old when I first heard your name.

. . .

Yes, I was raised loving you—at least the idea of you.

. . .

Where do I begin? Am I in charge of my life? Are you calling the shots? Is this life preordained? Does the past have only one function: to predict the future?

I have to go back there now, to some point in the beginning, when I was small . . .

. . .

We stayed in Jacksonville Beach for a while after Daddy died. Didn't bother me none. I liked it there. I saw Daddy all the time. He walked around, kinda lonesome looking. He never did say anything, I guess 'cause he knew I was scared of the spirit world. But it did make me a little happy to know that he was still with us, even if I couldn't touch him, and he couldn't say, "How about a Slim Jim, sunshine!"

Mama and Deedee, they never saw him. They weren't open. They was too tied up in their own sadness to realize he hadn't left.

One day when Aunt Lil was visiting, her and Mama were drinking coffee, and I was playing with my Etch A Sketch, pretending like I wasn't listening, when Mama says, "I've got to take the girls away from here. Everywhere I turn, I'm reminded of him. I can't take it anymore."

That was my first hint that we were leaving Jax Beach. My second was when Mama called Deedee and me into the kitchen after Aunt Lil had left and told us she needed a fresh start.

She said, "Listen to me, we're moving to Tampa. They don't have the ocean there. Once we leave this place, we'll never hear the surf ever again. Can you handle that?"

I, for one, did not want to live where there weren't any waves to sooth my nerves, but Mama seemed set on heading out, so Deedee and me, trying to be good daughters, said, "The sound of the surf don't make any difference to us."

But it did. And maybe that was a bad lie.

I don't know why Mama picked Tampa. Maybe she wanted to punish us by taking us far away from the waves.

Anyway, that's why we're living in a trash heap of a travel trailer at a place called the Traveler's Motor Lodge.

I've nicknamed the trailer The Blister. That's what it looks like. Pale and round. I want to pop it.

It ain't no bigger than a Buick. It's not the kind of place a family can live in full time. But there you go. We do. It's got one bedroom. That's for Deedee and me. Mama sleeps on the ratty couch at the front, up at the hitch end.

Our new home is roach-infested. I hate them roaches. At night they line up on the door frame, waiting for me to go into the bedroom, and then they dive-bomb me.

Also, they bite. Every morning I wake up with red marks all over my arms and legs. Mama says they ain't biting, just nibbling a little bit.

Nebraska Avenue is full of whores. That's what Mama says. I asked her what a whore was, and she said, "None of your goddamn business."

But I think I know.

Besides, she's the one who said it.

There's lot's of bars on Nebraska, including a biker hangout. Mama told me never to go walking near there 'cause a man was killed out front two nights ago. Nearly right across the street is a pretty Pentecostal shack church where the Negroes go. Then there's the truck stop. That's about it. Bars, whores, truckers, churches.

We're flat broke. Mama does some bookkeeping and cleaning for Mr. Terrino. He owns this joint and he's pretty nice. Everybody says so. I believe them. But, still, I can't help myself—I'm a little afraid of him. Not 'cause he's bad or anything. I can't really say why. I'm getting kinda confused here, so let me tell you this part. He walks around singing Italian songs at the top of his lungs and makes us females laugh.

He's got three good-looking sons. I'd bet my titties that my sister is gonna have something going on with David before too long. I know all about goo-goo eyes.

Anyway, the thing is, our welfare check keeps us in beans, but that's about it. Mama hates being on welfare. In fact, she gets mad when I mention the very word.

She snaps, "We are not on welfare! It is Aid to Dependent Women and Their Children. Your father paid into that. We're not taking anything we haven't already given."

Mama is bad lonely without Daddy. At night, after Deedee and me have gone to bed, she sits out there on that couch and cries. She usually starts out soft and low but after a few drinks she gets pretty loud. Then after a few more drinks, she talks to him. Don't know if he's listening or not. I kinda hope not, 'cause she calls him bad names. But she almost always follows that up by telling him how much she loves him. The usual saint and sinner stuff.

I don't like it when Mama is upset. I've decided that since she's a poor, helpless widow, that it's my job to make her happy. So when she's out there on that couch having a crying jag, I get out of bed and go visit her. I pour her liquor and light her cigarettes, and she hangs on to me for pure life.

But sometimes she turns mean. She'll glare at me as if I'm the ugliest piece of trash she's ever laid eyes on, and she'll spit, "You look just like him. You make me sick!"

I admit, I do look like him. So when she says that I always say, "Sorry, Mama."

We ain't got a TV. But Mr. Terrino loaned us a transistor radio. It's the best! On Thursday nights, I listen to "Radio Mystery Theater." My imagination goes wild, letting the music and sound effects and all that create a moving picture

show in my head. I sure do like the way the story and everything works together.

But the radio does more than entertain me on Thursday
nights. See, like I said, Mama is bad lonesome. And her temper, it's getting worse and worse. Could be the Irish in her.
She beat the daylights out of me three nights ago 'cause I didn't
want to clean my plate. But I hate peas. She knows I hate peas.

She said, "You think you're so goddamn better than us!"

When I get big, I'm never eating another pea in my life.

But back to the radio. Every weekday for an hour, a show
comes on that Mama loves. She lets me sit with her on the
trailer steps while she listens. We drink iced tea together and
sometimes she laughs. It's sort of a girly laugh and that em-
barrasses me. And one other thing. Sometimes she listens
real closely, her head tilted, her cigarette lodged between her
knuckles. And then she'll nod as if she and that radio man
are in perfect agreement.

I like it when she listens to the radio man 'cause for those
few minutes out of Mama's old sad life, she seems sort of
happy. Not the kind of happy she was when her and Daddy
was getting along. But the kind of happy you feel when your
troubles don't weigh on your heart anymore like a sack of
rocks.

Today the radio man said something that Mama found
real funny. She giggled just like she used to when Daddy was
around, and she stared into the bright blue heat of the Tampa
sky and said so softly, just the way a person does when they

truly, truly mean what they're saying, "If I were a younger woman, I would marry that man."

.   .   .

BUT MAMA couldn't marry you. So I have, after a fashion.

.   .   .

HOW ODD IT IS that the idea of you—the witty, kind, erudite radio talk-show host who existed solely as a golden beacon in the silent light of Mama's imagination—was the last happy dream she ever had.

.   .   .

KATIE AND I pore over the pages you wrote today. We take our task seriously. I sit on the floor, the script in front of me, Katie resting her head in my lap. I'm a decent editor with good instincts. I make notes in the margins, suggestions for recasting some of the dialogue that seems stilted, keeping in mind that you're writing for a commercial audience and that my taste in literature has nothing in common with mass-market movie appeal. Also, I have to remember that I'm the student, you're the master. I'm supposed to be learning from you. It's a compliment, really, that you asked me to look at these pages at all.

· · ·

IT'S PAST MIDNIGHT when you finally waltz in. Katie and I have fallen asleep on the couch. She barks as you fiddle with your keys on the front porch. You are having a terrible time getting the key in the lock, so I get up to let you in.

You sway in the harsh glare of the porch light, and for an instant you look like my daddy. Him coming home smashed. Mama ordering him to take a shower, and then demanding that Deidre and me watch as he—stark naked—fumbles for a towel at the linen closet.

"Look at your father. What a loser. Henry, I want you to remember this in the morning. I hope you're ashamed of yourself, letting your two daughters see you like this."

Daddy giggled and continued to rummage through the closet. He did not know what was happening. Liquor had turned him into an innocent.

I felt sorry for him. And ashamed of myself. I should have refused to look. I should have taken Mama's wrath, redirected it away from Daddy, refused to have participated in her mean game.

So I look at you now, swaying helplessly in the moth-filtered light, and I think of my daddy and my shame, and any tendency I had to be angry at you evaporates in the awful heat of my past.

· · ·

You sleep late, and I have the day off so I give Katie a bath, all the while trying to figure out how to tell you our phone service was disconnected this morning.

Katie prefers to stay dirty (she hates baths), and I suspect that in her mind she thinks she is indulging just one more of my bizarre human whims. Even when I take a shower, she ventures into the bathroom and glances at me as if I'm off my rocker. Then she turns and walks out, and I swear sometimes I believe I've seen her shake her head as if to say, "Mama sure has some strange habits."

I rinse the soap out of her dense black fur, and then try to hang on to her so I can dry her off. But she slips my grip and heads straight for the sand pit in the backyard. I run after her and attempt to wrangle her back onto the porch. Katie is a loving dog, but she is also stubborn. Finally, I resort to picking her up, all forty-plus wet pounds of her. As I struggle back toward the house, you step outside, the pages I edited in hand.

"Hi," I say as Katie squirms. "I gave Katie a bath."

You're dressed in your nice linen pants and a blue cotton sports shirt. You are freshly showered. I can't put Katie down because she'll either jump on you and mark up your pants with dog paws, or run back to the sand pit.

You glare at me with narrowed eyes. I know I'm in trouble. I try to back away and still keep a grip on Katie, who is squirming like a giant worm. You ball up a page and fling it at me.

"You won't do this to me! You won't belittle my work!"

"I-I-I-I'm sorry! I guess I didn't know what I was doing. I didn't mean anything b-b-b-bad by it. I swear! You asked me to help!"

You throw another wad of paper. It hits Katie in the eye. She yelps. I pet her as I set her down. "You hurt Katie!"

"I didn't hurt the damn dog!"

I'm kneeling in the grass beside my dog, trying to determine if her eye is damaged.

You come closer, hurling more pages, one after the other.

"I've worked all my life to get to this point, and I'm not gonna let some little fool like you mess it up for me."

Run! Run now! That's what the voice in my head is screaming, but my legs will not cooperate. You are the snake. I am the child. Where are my keys? I have to take Katie with me. Scared of what you'll do if I leave her behind. I hold on to my dog as you approach. When you reach me you lean down, take me by my hair, and stuff a page in my mouth.

"Eat it, you no good bucktoothed bitch! Maybe you'll learn something!"

Then you shove my face to the ground.

Katie, of her own accord, inserts herself between us, licking the arm that I shield myself with.

This is how I remain—huddled in the dirt with Katie acting as my protectress—until I hear the perfectly timed engine of your silver Audi purr to life, and I'm certain you've sped away.

.   .   .

KATIE IS CALM. Katie is good. She knows I'm upset. She sticks right by my side, brushing up against me, letting me know she's there.

We get into my Torino. I haven't any destination in mind. We're just going for a drive, trying to settle my nerves. I don't know what's happening. I don't have a life, just a series of mistakes.

I should have never agreed to help you. I don't know enough. I don't know anything.

We head down Bayshore. Katie lifts her nose to the breeze. She appears divine. Full of knowledge. What does the wind tell her? Does she know what the rich people ensconced in their Bayshore mansions are having for lunch? Does she know what kind of pets they own? Does she know if they are good people or bad? Dying or healthy? Selfish or giving?

I rub her ears and wish that I possessed her sense of smell. For a few hours or a day. But maybe humans would go crazy. Sensory overload. Or maybe the heightened knowledge would make us nicer, propelling us to view the world as a complex, dynamic event rather than a continuum chock-full of roadblocks.

My horn doesn't have a cap over it. The wires stick out of the steering column and, despite my best efforts, they sometimes rub together, which produces a spark and causes the horn to honk. Drivers who think I'm honking at them shoot me dirty looks.

What's worse is if I need to use the horn, because then I

have to take both hands off the wheel and touch the wires together.

Today, though, as we spark and honk our way down the road, Katie barks at each unexpected blast. And I begin to laugh. And the taste of paper and ink recedes.

I make a right turn onto Gandy. We could head across the bridge and go to the causeway. Or we could travel west until the road runs out and all there is to see is the Gulf. We could sit on the beach and listen to the surf. The Gulf isn't as loud as the Atlantic, but it's still nice. Very calming. Katie and I could go for a walk. She could poop in the sand. She could chase gulls.

But no. I'd better stay close to home. My car, it might not make it across the bridge. The radiator will blow. The tires will blow. The shot ball-joints will blow.

I stop at Wendy's and buy Katie a hamburger at the drive-through window. I feed it to her in the parking lot, keeping the pickles for myself. As Katie wolfs down her treat, I say, "You and me are in a heck of a mess, little girl. We're gonna be out on the street soon."

What I need, I realize, is five hundred bucks. That's what it will take, minimum, to get us into a new apartment. First and last months' rent, damage deposit, electricity, phone. Maybe I can sell the car. No, not the car. How would I get to work? How would I get away? Besides, who'd pay actual money for this heap? I hug Katie and give her a big smooch on her muzzle. *Think, Connie. Think your way out of this!*

I fire up the Torino and drive. Again. Aimlessly. I travel the side streets, looking at the pretty houses, imagining myself living in one someday. Really, I'm just meandering, and that's why I am surprised when I find myself in front of the battered women's shelter. Actually, it's not far from my apartment. Just a few blocks. And there's a parking space right there. I pull into it and look at the front door. The place looks real nice, not threatening at all. I could march in there and offer my services as a volunteer. I would tell them about Mama's sad life and that I'm doing this for her. Sort of like penance. This would be good for me, helping others instead of thinking about my own troubles. I could answer the phones. Maybe just a couple of nights a week. Right now, this very minute, I could leave Katie in the car while I go in and ask for volunteer information. *No, I can't stay. My dog is in the car.* They probably have a brochure about how to volunteer. And a training program. What would that be like, I wonder, talking to battered women on the phone, trying to get them to safety? I don't have a clue. I'd probably be terrible at it. I don't have the kind of backbone it takes to help women like that. I really don't understand them.

I slip the Torino in gear and speed away.

.   .   .

BEFORE I GET HOME, my right front tire blows. This is not unusual. They blow all the time, from the shot ball-joints, see. So I drive on my rim to the convenience store around the corner from the apartment. People glare because I'm making so much noise. I have no choice. I don't have a spare and wouldn't know how to change a tire if somebody gave me one for free. I'll have to call my brother-in-law. He is used to coming out and fixing my car.

He'll say, "You shouldn't be driving on the rim."

And I'll just shrug my shoulders because I don't know what else he expects me to do.

Okay, what are my priorities? Get a tire. That has become the new number one. The new number two is try to talk the landlord into giving us a break. And number three is try to work some extra shifts so that we can get the phone turned back on.

. . .

"What if I paid you more rent per month? Would you let us stay then?" The convenience store is bustling. White people. Black people. Spanish people. Kids. Adults. Everybody stopping in to get a quick fix of cigarettes or cold drinks or candy bars. It's difficult to hear on this pay phone, but I manage to make out my landlord's response.

"Lady, you could pay me double, plus all the back rent, and get rid of that hound of yours, and I'd still kick you out."

"But I can pay you. It will just take a little while. I was in the hospital. I didn't realize my roommate wasn't paying the rent. I'm the one who usually pays. He didn't know. It was an honest mistake."

"Look lady, you've got two weeks. That's it. If it was up to me, you'd already be out of there. But the law looks out for your kind."

I want to ask him, What kind is that? But I know what he means. It was on the tip of his tongue. White trash. Lazy dumb-asses who get their phones turned off for non-payment. Idiots without health insurance. Ne'er-do-wells who will never amount to squat, so why don't we just die and leave the rest of society in peace.

As I hang up, the man waiting in line behind me says, "You got a quarter? I need to call home and don't have any change."

I rummage through my Crown Royal bag and hand him the money. "A bartender always has change," I tell him.

.   .   .

"We need five hundred dollars."

I tell you this when you return two days later, behaving as if you'd never thrown a fit or tried to force me to eat paper and ink. You do not apologize for your actions or explain your whereabouts. This is fine with me. I don't want to know where you have been. My one consuming concern is that we'll be put out on the street. I've been homeless before—lived in my Torino for a month when an old room-mate took off on me. But now I have Katie. The two of us can't make it in my car. So this fear of total dispossession, for a few moments, empowers me. I must make you understand.

Five hundred dollars.

Amazingly, instead of responding to my statement, you come on to me. You push me against the wall and rub your hand down my cheek. I pull away.

"I mean it. I just talked to the landlord. Even if we pay him double, he won't rescind the eviction notice. We're really screwed."

You slump down into your cinnamon-colored easy chair. You light a cigarette and look at me through the smoke.

"I'm not finding five hundred dollars for you. That's final. If you want it so bad go out on the street and hustle it."

"It's not for me. It's for us. Without it, we won't have a place to live."

"Fuck you."

I look at you sitting there with your cigarettes and your defiant old face, and I realize that I'm drowning. What am I not saying? What am I not explaining? Why do I suspect I'm going mad?

"Well, you know, I suppose Katie and I can live in the Torino for a while. Maybe one of your sons will take you in."

"Jesus fucking Christ, what do you want from me? Blood? You want me to call up my guys and tell them some broad wants five hundred bucks? I'm not borrowing money for you. Look, here, here!"

You pick up your address book and start flipping through it, throwing various names at me—the mayor, a former governor, an ex–beauty queen—taunting me as to whom you should call. You reach for the phone and put it to your ear.

"What the fuck! What's wrong with the phone?"

"They turned it off."

"You stupid bitch! What am I supposed to do now? I've got deals working out there. I've got to have a phone."

You stand and start to pace, pulling your fingers through your hair. You kick the small table the phone is on, and the whole thing topples over.

"You bitch!" you repeat, and then with one hand you nail me to the wall.

I want to say, "If you want a phone that works then pay for it!" but I know better. "Let go of me!"

"What? What's wrong? Are you scared?"

I look past him—never in his eyes—and say quietly, "Let me go."

"Let me go!" you mock, pinning me with greater force.

You take a slow drag off your cigarette.

I turn my head as you blow the smoke in my face.

You study the cigarette for a moment as if it's an object of exquisite beauty, and it is then I know I'm fucked. I try again to squirm away, but you are much stronger than you look. You bring the cigarette to my cheek.

I close my eyes. If I don't watch, maybe it won't hurt, maybe it won't happen. I feel it in the hollow of my cheek, a red, stinging scream of a pain as you stub the cigarette out on my skin while saying slowly, giving each word equal weight, "You stupid cunt."

Katie is at my feet. She barks and whines and stamps her feet. I think she smelled my burning flesh before I did.

"Tell your fucking dog to shut up."

You flick the butt onto the floor. Then you slump back into your chair and turn on the TV.

"Go get me a beer."

My impulse is to scream at you. To beat on you. To shout that you are a filthy swine.

But, of course, I don't do that. Of course, I go into the kitchen and get a Michelob. And of course, I hold the cold aluminum can to my burned skin.

.   .   .

I PUT ON MY very best outfit. I cover my bruises with foundation. I dab concealer on the wound on my face. I flinch as I touch my burned skin. Makeup really doesn't cover a burn— it just makes it sting worse.

Then I get in my Torino with the bald tire Phil put on just yesterday, and I drive to the Barnett Bank downtown. I am real nervous. I try to summon confidence. I try to appear calm, trustworthy. But even my palms are sweaty.

I am trying to soothe my fears by studying the sculpted patterns in the carpet when the loan officer calls my name. I stand unsteadily on my black high heels and wobble over.

She indicates that I am to sit. So I do. She has a big desk. And it's very neat. No clutter. Everything in its place. I glance at her. She is a bottle blonde. Probably in her forties. Pretty.

And very, very cold. She's her own private iceberg. I can tell that from how manicured she is. People who are warm usually don't look like a mannequin.

"What can I do for you today?"

I tell her I would like to apply for a loan. For five hundred dollars.

Her pink lips drop open. Her heavily shadowed lids flutter. Then she throws back her head and laughs.

"We don't give five-hundred-dollar loans. The least amount we lend is five thousand. And I don't think you want that. Do you." This is a statement. Not a question.

I am mortified. I think I might burst into tears. If I try to speak, I definitely will. So I sit there, like an idiot, silent.

"If all you need is five hundred dollars, I recommend you ask your parents. Now, is there anything else I can do for you?"

.   .   .

WE HAVE A MUTUAL FRIEND who suffers from muscular sclerosis. He's the only one of your buddies whom I truly respect. He doesn't try to brandish his power. He doesn't have any. He lives simply. He isn't flush like your other pals. He drives an old beat-up Japanese car, and I'm sure he watches what he spends at the supermarket. If he goes to the movies, it's only to the matinees. And after paying his monthly mortgage, he probably resents bankers and dimes.

So you can imagine how useless I feel when he shows up

at the apartment with a check written to me for five hundred dollars, saying that you told him I had to have the money. That I wouldn't be happy until I had the money. That he had to do this for you so that I'd get off your back. It's all about the money and my greed and my troubled ways. It's all on me.

You've turned yourself into victim-hero. Again.

"I'm doing this for him," he says. "I don't know what kind of trouble you've gotten yourself into, but you'd better pay me back. I don't have money to throw around."

I try to explain that it's not just for me, that it's not some frivolous whim. But he won't listen. He holds up his hand to silence me.

"I don't want to hear it. Like I said, I'm doing it for him. Not you."

And now I want to know, What did you say to him? What lies? What sick light did you cast me in?

I should have ripped up the check. I should have never accepted it. Pride should have taken over.

But it didn't.

As he leaves he touches his cheek as a way to indicate the burn mark on my face and says, "By the way, you ought to have that impetigo looked at."

.   .   .

I'M BACK AT THE phone booth telling more lies.

"There is trouble with the lines. Our whole street is without service," I tell my prospective employer.

"We were wondering what the problem was. We've been trying to reach you for two days."

"I'm sorry. I should have called sooner, but I didn't want you to think I was rushing you."

"Not at all. We were worried as to how to reach you."

And then, just as though I have a normal life consistent with the rules of decent society, the woman offers me the job. "We all agreed you were far ahead of the other applicants."

I can't believe it. I want to shout, "Yes!"—but I figure that's not professional. I start crying, but she can't see me so what the hell! A woman in shorts walks past and shoots me a concerned look.

"I'm so glad . . . That's so wonderful. Um . . . when do I start?" I say, trying to keep at bay my trembling voice.

I do not walk home. I float. I am unbelievably happy. I can't wait to give notice at Bennigan's. I can't wait to be a real professional in a job people respect. *I'm an editor.* I try on the words. They feel terrific. They fit like a handmade suit. I burst into the apartment.

"Guess what! I got the job!"

You look up from the book you're reading, something by Larry King, and you flash me that "Hey, are we fabulous, or what?" grin. You pull me down beside you and kiss me and say, "I knew you could do it, kiddo! I just knew it!"

That evening we giggle and drink and make plans. The mark on my cheek is nearly healed. The rings of Saturn have grown faint. Katie stretches out beside me, relaxed and, I think, happy at our playful chatter.

You get up to use the bathroom. I nuzzle Katie's neck.

"K-K-K-Katie!" I sing softly. And then I whisper in her ear, "This is it, little girl. Everything will get better from here on out."

. . .

DID FATE BRING us together? Or is life simply a series of events, some of which will undoubtedly echo stirrings from the past?

I cannot decide. My opinion changes with the rapidity of light, depending on my level of cynicism at any given moment.

However, in the wake of being offered a real job by people who do not know I have a connection to you and who awarded me the position based solely on my own merit and hard work and perceived talent, I can't help but reconsider the odd circumstances in which we met.

I mean, it was for a reason. Wasn't it?

. . .

MAMA HAS BEEN DEAD for two months.

For sixty days no one has yelled at me or called me stupid, or accused me of being an ungrateful whore or a lousy excuse for a daughter.

No one has said, "I wish to God I had died the day you were born!"

Despite this progress, I am profoundly unhappy. I want to go to sleep and never wake. But dying is more difficult than I dreamed it would be. The body does not stop functioning easily. Death is a time-consuming process, unless it's a bullet through the brain. And even then, who knows what messages, words, images are telegraphed by exploding synapses and neurons? I want to know, when you're dying how long does a second last?

So much for self-pity. I'm still alive. And Mama's still dead. And it's a new semester. I'm sitting in the back of the classroom, my head down on the desk, waiting for the prof to show up.

I used to look forward to the start of classes. Now the only thing I look forward to is sleep. It's practically the only thing I do. I don't go to parties or bars or restaurants. I'm in danger of losing my on-campus job because I no longer give a damn about proper filing or phone answering or message taking.

The registrar picked my classes for me this term. I told her, "Just put me down for something. I can't decide."

If I had been in my right mind and, therefore, capable of making my own decisions, I would have never chosen this class. Screenwriting 101. Professor to be announced. I am a poet. Not a hack who churns out stale dialogue for mass consumption.

Maybe I should drop the class. But then I'd have to wander around campus, getting the right forms and signatures. It might be easier to just sit this out.

"Young lady, you with your head on the desk, can you please turn down the air conditioner before it starts snowing in here?"

I must be losing it. I remember that voice. I used to listen to it every afternoon back in my trailer days. This is too weird. It would be like a miracle or something. I look up. And there you are. A gift from heaven. That's my sense of things.

"The air conditioner? Turn it down?"

I stand up and fiddle with the AC controls. You introduce yourself to the class. I sense Mama's hand in all this. *"If I were a younger woman I would marry that man."*

Oh Mama, if only you were here now, you would be absolutely thrilled. You died too soon. Here he is, in the flesh, the radio man you once swooned over. And I'm his student! If you were still alive, I would run home and tell you who my professor is and you'd slap your thigh and say, "Hot-dog!"

You wouldn't call me a stupid bitch anymore.

You wouldn't ridicule me for the hours I spend reading and writing.

No, if you knew about this, your dying words—which I can't speak or even allow myself to remember right now— would be in a whole different tune.

. . .

YOU HAVE TO ADMIT, given the background information, it is odd. I mean, Mama's infatuation with you, and then, without my even trying, when I'm at my most vulnerable, you walk into my life.

Fate? Chance? Providence? Luck?

Mama always said, "Paybacks are hell."

. . .

THE NEWSPAPER'S PUBLISHER takes me to lunch. To get to know me better. She wants to be my friend. She wants me on her side. This tiny, fledgling publication is thick with family intrigue. Old husbands. New wives. Ex-friends. All fighting over position, power, money. Which I find slightly curious since this rag of a paper isn't turning a profit and can barely claim a circulation.

But that's all right. That's why they hired me. Someone just starting out. Someone cheap and hungry, with a vulnerability that each editorial board member senses they can use to their own advantage.

We are barely halfway through our croissant chicken-salad sandwiches, and I already know that she hasn't always been strictly a housewife and part-time publisher. She used to be a social worker—that could work in my favor. Aren't social workers kind, understanding and helpful?

"Social work," I say, "what a wonderful field."

I'm trying to behave as if I'm mature and confident and capable of having an adult conversation. Because the pending eviction dominates my waking and sleeping hours, and because my new job requires that I drive my terribly unde-pendable heap many miles in heavy traffic across the bay to a neighboring county, I express a desire to move from Tampa to St. Petersburg.

"The drive over the bridge is so awful. Especially at rush hour. I think I'll do a much better job if I'm close to the office."

"I agree. That bridge is simply too dangerous."

She pauses as if she has just been struck by brilliance. She empties a packet of Sweet'N Low into her coffee and thoughtfully stirs before saying, "You know, I have a rental property that just became vacant. I wasn't planning on rent-ing it until some repairs were finished. But, maybe we could talk about it."

I do not dare draw a breath for several seconds. I try to keep my face steady. I try not to shout, "Hallelujah!"

What does one do when a near-stranger unknowingly makes a lifesaving offer? Would it be inappropriate to jump up and hug her? Or to start bawling and in between my heav-ing tears mumble, "Thank you, thank you, thank you!"? Or to spill my guts about my desperate straits, as if she's some long-lost girlfriend?

That wouldn't do. Not at all. This is my employer. I must remain professional. I've come too far to make a boob of my-self now.

But what if it's too expensive? What do I do then? "Sorry, but I can't afford it"? That would be mortifying. But hold on, she set my salary. She knows I'm not bringing down the big bucks. Just go for it. Say something positive. I fold my hands neatly in my lap as my mind falls all over itself. *Say something, stupid!*

Finally I do.

I look up from my coffee. "Is it nearby?"

.   .   .

THERE ARE confessions to make.

I have a dog. And no credit rating. And I live with someone whose name you will recognize, whose face will be familiar to you—and, yes, he is old enough to be my father.

"Is he still on the radio?"

"No, he quit."

"To do what?"

"Write screenplays."

"Oh?"

"Yes. He's very successful."

.   .   .

THE HOUSE IS A 1930s bungalow in a nice neighborhood complete with sidewalks. We're three blocks from the bay and five minutes from my new office. We have a wide front screened porch, part of which has been turned into a sunroom with French doors that lead into the bedroom. The living room is large and white and has built-in cabinets. The kitchen is at the very back of the house and has a door to the outside. The bathroom is small, grungy, but I don't mind. Even with the grunge, this place is the finest digs I've ever lived in.

The best part of all is that a dog run parallels the length of the house, so Katie has a secure place to sit in the sun. Even so, she prefers the porch. She sits atop the wooden table, which I pulled out of a stranger's garbage one midnight, and observes life. She scares the bejesus out of unassuming passersby. I'm pretty sure she enjoys those brief moments of ferocious barking and the startled expressions on the humans' faces. I think it's her idea of a joke.

Katie likes this house. Her personality is blooming. She runs from room to room as if in awe of our increased square footage. She has begun to prance, and I take this to be a sign of her growing confidence. She brings me her ball and sock and the old running shoe I gave her three months back. If she wants attention, she'll stamp her front feet, lift her head like a wolf, and bark.

I always respond by saying, "Why, Miss Katie, what is it you want, little girl?" She barks again and then flashes me that beautiful canine aw-shucks grin.

It is then that I get on the floor and wrestle with her and hug her and let her lick my face. I hear laughter in the room and am surprised that it's coming from me. In these precious minutes, Katie and I regain our innocence.

. . .

You phone me at the office, your voice buoyant, to tell me you have gotten me a gift.

"What is it?" I ask, fearing you have stolen again.

"If I told you it wouldn't be a surprise. Let's just say, it's bigger than a bread box. And it hasn't even begun yet!"

"You're talking in riddles."

"Come home, Constance. Now."

I pause before answering. I cannot come home now. I have a deadline to meet. I don't want to mess up this job. I have a chance here, a real chance, to begin to cobble together a life. But I can't tell you that. You would explode.

So I say, "I'll be there as soon as I can."

. . .

To my own amazement, I don't rush home. I keep working, pasting down the layout for the next issue, all the while trying to beat back a growing sense of dread about what might await me at home. The sensation starts in my feet and edges up, up, up, until I can barely breathe. But I will not give in. I have a job to do. You cannot call all the shots. It's high time I grew up, I tell myself.

I take my pasted-up boards over to IO Graphics. It's a mom-and-pop operation run by a very kind couple named Heather and George. They do all my typesetting and art work. They are older than me, but not by much. They have long hair and lots of cats. I think maybe we can be friends. I would like that.

In fact, they ask me to stick around. Maybe have a glass of wine. Perhaps catch dinner later.

I can't. I can't. I'm really sorry. I have to get home.

.   .   .

THIS IS THE FIRST TIME I've ever disobeyed you. I should have been home hours ago. Maybe you will be asleep. Maybe you will have forgotten.

No such luck. You are waiting for me on the porch. I'm afraid to get out of my car. My scalp begins to ache. I must be anticipating you yanking me by the hair. I keep my eyes averted as I make the long walk from the car to the house.

"There you are, darling," you say. "I was worried about you."

"I had to get some things done."

"Of course."

You open the screen door for me. I step inside. You tell me to shut my eyes. I don't want to shut my eyes. I need to be able to properly gauge when to shield my face. But I have no power here. Just take the blow. It will be over soon.

"Hold out your arms."

I hear a door open and scuffling noises and then you place something soft, furry, and squirming in my arms. I open my eyes. It's a golden retriever puppy you have taken the liberty of naming God.

"A joke on dyslexics," you say with sauced glee, leaning against the door frame and beaming.

Who, except for a jerk, could resist a puppy's charms? Certainly not me.

"You are so adorable! Yes, you are!" I coo. "Just look at that puppy belly!"

"Well, Constance, you and that mutt of yours are so close, I figured I needed a dog of my own to even things out."

I let the pup chew on my finger. I rub his fat little belly and ask, "Where's Katie?"

"I've got her locked in the back room. Didn't want her hurting God."

"Katie's not gonna hurt this little guy! She wouldn't hurt a fly!"

As I pick up the puppy and brush past, you say lightly, the threat gleaming, "She'd better not."

. . .

KATIE AND THE PUPPY are tussling in the living room. He already outweighs her and is far more aggressive in play than she is. So there is not much sport to this game. He pins her repeatedly, ignoring her yips and cries.

I break them up but you say, "Oh, let him play!"

"He was getting too rough with her."

"Then maybe she'll learn to stay away from him."

I kneel down and pet Katie. She presses against me and licks my face. The pup bounds over and pushes her away, desiring all the attention.

"Kate, come here. Come here, sweetie." She eyes the big

blond dog whose exuberance reveals itself in every excited hop, nip, and playful tug. With her head lowered, she walks over to the corner and slumps down.

He's just a puppy, I remind myself. All puppies are attention hogs. I watch him play with a rubber hamburger squeak toy. From the rear view it would appear that his testosterone level is anything but lacking. I don't want Katie being put in a situation where she must be submissive. I understand that all this may be normal dog psychology, the alpha male and all that, but Katie is giving in without even a hint of a fight. Which might not bother me so much, except she seemed so much happier and self-confident before the puppy came along.

"Maybe," I say, rubbing the pup's ears, "we need to think about getting him fixed."

You jerk your head toward me, and I instinctively draw back. You sneer through your cigarette smoke.

"What? You want two emasculated males in the house? Fuck off, lady."

.   .   .

YOU ARE SOBERING UP. That's what you claim. We're having dinner at a French restaurant near the house, and you tell the waiter not to even present the wine list. You say things are going too well with your latest project (another screenplay) for liquor to be clouding your judgment. You've gone to a doctor, a pal of yours, and he has prescribed Antabuse.

"What is it?"

"Behavior modification," you say, lighting a cigarette and then reaching for a glass of ice water. "You drink while taking this stuff, and it will nearly kill you."

"What do you mean?"

"I mean, if I take a drink, it'll make me so sick I'll wish I was dead."

"Is it dangerous?" I think this is a harmless question. But there are no harmless questions between us. I should know that by now.

You slam your fist onto the table. Your water sloshes and our fellow patrons turn and glare. I'm sure they think I'm your daughter. You lean toward me, and through clenched teeth say, "You don't know me, lady. You have no idea what I can do once I set my mind to it."

.   .   .

I LIVE TWO LIVES NOW.

At home I am submissive. I try to read your moods. I try not to say anything that will catapult you into a rage. I try not to be stupid.

At work, I am expected to be aggressive, creative, poised. I deal with advertisers and printers and photographers and freelance writers. I hire and I fire. I hold meetings. I interview important people. F. Lee Bailey, Chesterfield Smith, Alex Haley. This takes a lot of energy on my part. I don't want anyone to know that I'm a fraud. I don't want them to know that sometimes my dog and I hang out in the bathroom with the door locked, waiting for you to fall asleep, divining the moment we'll be safe again. I don't want them to dismiss me simply on the basis of my buckteeth. I think my teeth reveal sordid secrets. They telegraph my past. They make me look poor and goofy. So I try extra hard to make sure that every article I edit and every layout I design and every story I write exceeds my publisher's standards. I record each interview and take copious notes. I don't reuse or erase the audio tapes. I keep them in a pile on my desk at home. I might be able to do something else with them one day. The information recorded on those tapes proves I am not stupid.

Which person is the real me? The young professional? Or the cowed little girl who has become a battered woman?

Maybe they are both real, and they're battling it out inside me.

This is my fear: that the battered woman will win. That she'll show up one day at the office and reveal herself to the shock and revulsion of my colleagues.

And then this wayward attempt to transform myself will all be over.

.   .   .

YOU HAVEN'T HAD a drink in four days. I think there might be hope. You're quiet. Pensive. You're revising a screenplay.

Some folks in Hollywood actually sound interested in it. You are renting a lot of movies. And sleeping. Sometimes you punch the air with your fists, and I don't know whether you're pretending or if your sleep is truly that troubled.

.　.　.

KATIE NO LONGER has a fruitful life. The new pup dominates her totally.

I take her for walks by herself, and sometimes we go for drives. But she's not the same. Even when she sniffs the wind, drawing from it its secrets, she does so with a tentativeness that breaks my heart.

.　.　.

"THAT IS NOT the proper way to cut an onion!"

"What? I'm just dicing it."

"No, you're not. You're fucking it up."

I pause, the knife raised. How much force would it take to plunge the blade into your heart? Do I have the strength? Or would you take it from me, laughing, and then cut my face?

"Do not serve me anything but the heart of the onion. That's the only part of this vegetable that you are to use. Do you understand?"

"What's wrong with the outer layers?"

"They're trash, you stupid slut. Do I have to teach you everything?"

. . .

In an effort not to drink, you are taking a nap. It is late afternoon, and I am trying to fix one of Mama's specialties: chicken and dumplings. My hands are deep in sticky dough, and I'm wishing I had called my sister for advice before I mixed the flour with water and created such a mess, when Katie starts barking. Earlier, I put her and the pup in the run, but it sounds as if she's at the front of the house.

"Not again!" I mutter. I'm afraid she'll wake you. I don't want you to yell at her. Or me. Two days ago you kicked at her, but I got between you and took the blow. I've got a shiner the size of a baseball on my shin. I grab a dishrag and wipe my hands as I head to the front door.

Katie stands at the base of the steps, wagging her tail, looking ever so pleased with herself. This is her third escape this week.

"How are you getting out, Miss Katie? Come on, come inside the house."

She smiles, gains the steps without hesitation, follows me into the kitchen, and heads straight for her water bowl.

"Thanks for not running away, Kateland."

. . .

You eat your dinner in silence.

Not drinking, I think, is killing you.

When you're done, you push back your bowl and say, "You know, kiddo, why don't you get your goddamn teeth fixed? You look like an idiot."

.   .   .

THERE ARE THINGS you don't know.

I'd rather be pummeled by your fists than your words.

Sometimes I say that I'm working late, but really I'm visiting Heather and George.

I have a secret savings account. I started it when I got my first paycheck. When I have enough saved up, I'm going to get braces.

I'm not going to look like this forever.

But I'm not going to get my teeth straightened because you call me names. I'm going to do it because I have a decent job now. I interview interesting, accomplished people. They answer my questions as if I have all the right in the world to ask them.

You just wait and see, things are going to change around here.

.   .   .

I BOUGHT A CAR TODAY. You were real nice about it. You said that my old heap made me look trashy. You took me to see your oldest son, who works at one of those big-time dealerships with all the shiny flags flying. You negotiated the deal for me. They gave me five hundred bucks for the Torino!

So that's why I'm tooling around town in a 1972 maroon Triumph two-seater flop top. It's a speedy little car. I bet I get some tickets.

I sort of miss the Torino—I take a corner tight and fast, the wind blows my hair asunder, and the stereo is cranked— but probably not for long.

.   .   .

A CHI-CHI DOWNTOWN boutique has loaned me a tight black number with a gold sash cinching my hips. They aren't offering me this out of the kindness of their hearts but because the magazine is giving them free advertising. It's all part of our three-year anniversary special issue. The publisher insists on a big splash. She wants to feature the editorial board and founders on the cover, all of us outfitted in rented tuxes and high-style cocktail dresses.

I look at myself in the store's three-paneled mirror. I wish I could keep the dress. Just as a souvenir or to wear to a nice party, if we ever went to one.

When the saleslady isn't watching, I look at the price tag. Yikes, way out of my range.

I strike a pose. Feet at the two o'clock position. Chest back. Stomach in. Head tilted ever so slightly. We learned this in phys ed in eighth grade. Also, how to sit with our legs crossed. I smile. Radiantly. And then I shut my eyes and imagine myself whole.

. . .

THE SITUATION IS THIS: I'm fucked. In five hours the founders and editorial board of this rag are meeting at the Don Cesar Resort—the famed Pink Palace—on St. Pete Beach to have our picture taken, and my publisher has ordered me (for reasons only she knows) to fire our photographer.

I asked the obvious. "Can I wait until after the shoot tonight and after we have the photographs in hand?"

"No! Fire him now! Find someone else!"

My secretary and I have worked the phones for the past hour trying to locate a replacement photographer. No one, it would appear, is willing to take the job on such short notice. Several sounded offended that we would even ask. I am learning the hard way that professional photographers are a temperamental lot.

It is nearly one-thirty. I have run through the Pinellas County yellow pages. And the Hillsborough County yellow pages. I have combed through the Rolodex.

To hell with it.

"I'm leaving," I tell my secretary. "I'm taking the boards over to IO."

Which is what I do. With my mock-up of next month's issue balanced in my hands, I push open the door with my foot.

George looks up from his typesetting machine and says,

"Oh, Connie, I'm glad you're here. I have a photographer for you."

"You do? Really?"

"Yes. And he's a good friend of Heather's and mine. He just got back into town. He's been on the West Coast. Shall I call him?"

"Well . . . yeah!"

George punches in the number and hands me the phone.

I am a little rattled. I've spent my entire morning trying to find a photographer, and George offers me one out of the blue?

"Hello?"

"This is Mika."

"Hi, Mike."

"No. Mika."

"Oh. Well, Mika, umm . . ."

I don't know what to say next. There's something about his voice that has inexplicably sent my stomach spinning. But in a good way.

"See, I am with this magazine. It's about computers, but it's not really, and I need a photographer. Tonight."

He asks a few questions. Color or black and white? Location? Time? He sounds sure of himself. Unruffled. I don't feel as if he's manipulating me at all. He's just asking rational questions for which he needs rational answers.

"Okay, I'll be there. I'll be the guy wearing the red tie."

"Good. Good. I'll see you then."

"At four-thirty. The light will be good then."

"Right."

I hand the phone back to George who hangs it up. I feel flushed. I don't understand how the sound of a stranger's voice can knock me off kilter. Maybe I need to eat. Maybe I've got low blood sugar.

"George, did my publisher call you?"

"No. Is she going to?"

"I don't think so."

George looks at me with squinted eyes, as though he's trying to determine what's going on in my head but he's too polite to come right out and ask. I know he'll get Heather on it later.

I grip the counter. I feel disoriented. As if I'm falling, but I'm not. I can't get his voice out of my head. Or his name. Mika. Mika. I love that name. It's so, so Old World but kind of arty. I wonder if it's his real name. I sure hope so. I feel ecstatic. And scared. How is this possible? I must be crazy. I'm swooning. Maybe I didn't get enough sleep, or maybe I'm getting the flu. When I'm sick I tend to blow stuff out of proportion. *Calm down. I am an editor. I needed to hire a photographer. This is what I do. This is my job. George just helped me out. That's all.* But how could my dilemma have been so easily solved without anyone's cognizant effort? Explain that!

"Did you know I fired Greg this morning?"

"Did you really? No, I didn't know. Well, it's certainly a good thing Mika is back in town."

And George laughs as, I'm learning, he always does when he perceives that the planet has stopped its wobbly spin long enough for us mortals to glean the benefits of a universe in perfect balance.

.   .   .

SEVERAL DAYS AGO the publisher decided to include you in the group photograph. She has started referring to you as our consultant. She must think you're still famous.

.   .   .

COCOONED IN THE beautiful silver skin of your Audi, we speed toward the Gulf of Mexico and the Don Cesar. You appear dashing in your rented tux. I bet people think we are rich. Maybe even happy.

.   .   .

YOU ARE AT THE BAR nursing a soda water with lime, and I am hovering near the lobby entrance so that I can corral our party, when the photographer, Mika, walks into the lavish central hall of the Don Cesar wearing not a red tie, but red tennis shoes.

He is slim. His skin is beautifully pale—like ivory—it is the skin women wish they had. He is of medium height. His hair and eyes are brown, and he wears wire-rimmed glasses. He is SO handsome. He looks like an artist, an intellectual, as if he's sensitive without being a sap. I decide he looks like

Sartre. I decide he can do anything he wants. If he tells us to stand on our heads, we will stand on our heads.

He is a calm photographer. He doesn't shout orders or yell, "Say cheese!" He seems like a no-nonsense kind of guy whose sole interest is in the work and not in impressing us.

"No, no, a little closer together. Connie, you're hidden. Can you please stand in front? Good. Good. Perfect."

As for me, I'm thinking, *He has a great butt.* And, *His nose—I love his nose—it's absolutely perfect.* And, *Look at the way he handles that camera, the way he gazes through the viewfinder, focusing on us, seeing ourselves in a way we cannot.*

No one knows I'm thinking these thoughts. And no one ever will. I have found a secret fantasyland in which I am the sole inhabitant.

Throughout the shoot, I steer clear of you. I manage this by trying to behave as if I know what I'm doing. I am the editor-in-chief, after all. A working girl who doesn't have time for personal asides, who doesn't fantasize about men who work for her.

I'm thinking, *Maybe he likes smart, independent women. Act sophisticated. I bet that's what he goes for.*

Way before I want this night to end, while we're all standing there in our rented clothes, Mika looks up from the lens, starts rewinding his film, and says, "That's it. We're done."

"Are you sure?"

"I've got everything I need."

"Great."

I'm crushed. I look down at my shoes. They are borrowed, too. My feet hurt. *Stupid shoes. I bet this photographer never calls me. He probably doesn't want to work for us ever again. He's probably gay.*

Our little band of would-be models chat among themselves.

Mika fiddles with his equipment.

You pontificate.

No one listens. Not really.

I just stand there in my ritzy outfit, lecturing myself that this photographer is trouble. Trouble with a capital *T*. No, all caps. Underlined. Bold-faced. Trouble, trouble, trouble! I walk away from our group and hide behind a potted palm. I want to be alone. I hate everybody.

"Excuse me?"

"Yes?" *Oh my God. It's Trouble.*

"If you have the time and if you wouldn't mind, I'd like to take a few shots of you alone. For my portfolio."

Why on earth would you want to do that? I mean, my dress is nice but the rest of me is not fit for human eyes. Especially my teeth. Not these buckteeth. Are you joking? Or insane? Or, perhaps, horribly cruel?

This is what I think but wisely I don't say a word. Not at first. The truth is, I want to do it. I am so flattered. Maybe I'm dreaming. I don't want to be a fool. It's no fun being everyone else's joke. But I don't sense meanness in him. There's no sign of a cruel streak. I don't even sense any pressure. *Forget what I said about trouble. Still waters. Good waters.*

It is in this place, in the calm steady kindness of his eyes, that I discover the room to say yes.

"Are you sure?" He looks right at me, not past or through.

Yes, I am sure.

Even as we wander over to a quiet corner of the hotel's ornate lobby, I fear that I'm reading far too much into his character and that I am exhibiting one of my most stubborn traits: hopeless gullibility.

Quietly, he tells me where to stand and where to sit and where to look, and before I can flee from the building, I realize I am truly modeling for him. This isn't a difficult job. I mean, basically, I just stand or sit there. It's not like he's asking me to do multiplication tables. In fact, I'm feeling sort of pretty, and suddenly I can't believe this night is happening. I am Cinderella without all the baloney.

. . .

You, of course, are furious. And jealous. I hear all about it on the drive home.

"I don't trust that photographer." You spit the word *photographer* as if it's acid on your tongue.

"Why not?"

"I've been around the block a few times, kiddo. I've never met a photographer I could trust further than I could throw him." You pause, shaking your head as if you're an angry sage. "Just watch out. That's all I'm saying."

It has begun to lightly rain. I stare out into the dark, listening to the windshield wipers' steady cadence, knowing it's best if I do not respond.

"And that business with taking your photograph. Give me a break. He was just trying to manipulate you. He knows an easy mark when he sees one. Next thing I know, he'll be convincing you to take off your clothes. Even tonight he managed to make you look like a slut."

I look down at my pretty dress and run my hand along the length of its gold sash. I bring my wrist to my nose and sniff. The sample of Chanel No. 5 that I sprayed on at the mall still lingers. I remember Mika saying, "Good, good, okay, look here, into the camera." *Click-whir, click-whir.* There was no judgment. There was his eye and the camera and me. And for a few moments, someone was seeing something in me that was valuable. He was looking at me in a way no one else ever had.

So I turn and stare at you, and I realize what you do to me. Every day. Every night. Every moment you are alive. You steal my joy.

.   .   .

I AM FOURTEEN YEARS OLD, and I'm walking home from school with my friend Patty. I love Patty. She has nerve. And humor. And she and her family don't care that I'm poor. They treat me fair.

Every day on our way home we pass a doctor's office. An

orthodontist. Patty has noticed the way I pause in front of the office as if by hanging out there something good might happen for my teeth. But on this day she says, "Why don't we go in?"

"What? Why?"

"To see if we can't get you an appointment."

I would never do this on my own. I lack the gumption to even go inside a convenience store alone. But she is one of those special people whose courage at times is infectious.

So we go in and Patty pushes me up to the reception desk. I tell the nurse I want to make an appointment. She doesn't ask me what is wrong. It's obvious. She says the earliest the doctor can see me is in two weeks.

I hesitate.

"Perfect!" Patty says.

On the way home, I swear her to secrecy.

For the next fourteen days I hoard my lunch money and I mow lawns and I pilfer change from Mama's pocketbook and I borrow the rest from Patty. I'm starting to feel pretty excited. I think I'm gonna get my teeth fixed. I think the doctor will figure it all out for me, and Mama won't have any choice but to help once she hears the facts.

So we go to my appointment, but they won't let Patty stay with me in the exam room. I've never even been to a dentist before, so I'm scared out of my mind. The place smells like biology class when we're dissecting frogs and earthworms. I sit in the big medical chair that reminds me of Captain Kirk's throne in "Star Trek," waiting for the doctor to come in, trying to stay strong, concentrating on how decent looking I'll be with good teeth. It's cold in here. You must have to be darn smart to make all these gadgets work.

It's a long wait. Just me and these weird dental tools and my shame. Embarrassment is the only thing that prevents me from getting the hell out of here. I'm too shy to just walk out. So I'm stuck. I study a poster on the wall about plaque. Plaque looks like a Tasmanian Devil. His job is to root out all the teeth in the world. Finally I hear someone politely cough. It is the doctor. I suppose his cough is a warning for me to stop picking my nose or whatever. He walks over to my Captain Kirk chair. I size him up. He is brusque. He probably doesn't want me as a patient. Maybe he knows I'm poor. He resembles the father on "My Three Sons." Only younger.

"That's quite an overbite you've got, young lady. Let's take a look. Open wide."

I don't like opening wide. I don't like exposing what I have spent my entire life hiding. But I have put myself in this position where there is no choice.

He makes a few "Hmpf!" noises as he methodically pulls my cheeks away from my gums. He tells me to open and close and bite down. "Okay, move your bottom row from side to side."

I'm fighting back tears. I am so ashamed. I am a ridiculous person. It's not my fault my teeth are bucked. But maybe it is. Who knows?

Finally he is done. He takes off his gloves. His long face drops into a scowl that I interpret as disgust.

"Frankly," he says, "you've got a mess in there. I can't do a thing for you."

"But what about braces?"

He shakes his head. His thin lips fold in on themselves so that they are hidden, causing him to appear mouthless. I hope he's not thinking, *White trash.* "Braces aren't going to even begin to fix those teeth."

I feel as if I've been punched in the gut. He might as well have said, "There is no hope for you. You're going straight to hell."

As fast as I can, I'm out of the office and in the street. The people in the waiting room were a blur. I hope they die. Not really. It just feels good to be mad at them. Patty runs after me and catches up at the crosswalk. I'm trying so hard not to cry, not to turn this in on myself. But once I speak the words, "He says there's nothing he can do," the tears start hard and heavy, and Patty calls him a no good fucking asshole. I love that word *fucking.* She must know this because she says it again. "No good fucking asshole. I hope his dick falls off." So even though I am promising myself that I will never let another doctor humiliate me or poke around in my mouth, and though I am hurting bad, I start to laugh. And she laughs. And we can't stop. And I'm pleased as punch to realize what good medicine bad language truly is. And because we don't want to stop laughing, because we don't want to admit my hurt, every time boys from school pass us as we make our way home, we say, "No good fucking asshole. I hope your dick falls off."

.　.　.

THE CURSE THAT plagues me has just gotten meaner.

I have a crush on a married man.

I hate this. I must overcome these feelings.

We all knew our lives were changing, that night at the Don Cesar. The photographer was somebody we never expected. He possessed an ease, an assurance the rest of us lacked.

You hated him the moment you laid eyes on him.

But I'm even more ridiculous. I fell hard at the mere sound of his voice.

.　.　.

MIKA'S MARRIAGE, he claims, is falling apart due to fatigue. Specifically, his fatigue.

He explains this to me one afternoon in my office against the backdrop of water dripping from the leaky ceiling into a pail.

He says that for several years he has held two to three jobs simultaneously while she stays home, watching soaps and reading newspapers. Because of all the newspaper reading she does, she is very up on current affairs. He says she doesn't want to work, that she likes her life and doesn't care if he's exhausted.

I take note that the words *passion* and *love* are left out of his complaint. Maybe he and his wife have been together so long they are beyond all that. But how would I know? I don't feel it's even my place to ask. In fact, this conversation should not be taking place.

He takes off his glasses and rubs his hand lightly across his eyes. I know he is waiting for me to respond. But I am no home wrecker. Nor do I wear my heart on my sleeve. And while I'm head-over-heels for this guy, I'm in too deep with somebody else. I can't see my way out. And even if I could, there is no way I would open myself up to someone else until I know, without any shadow of a doubt, that he is not a monster.

I weigh my responses. I could say, "Hey, I've never been married so I can't help you," or, "I'm really the wrong person to tell this to because in my heart I'm a teenybopper blinded by love," or, "Listen, I'm trapped in the most screwed-up relationship in the world. You really don't want my advice."

But instead, as I watch him rub his right thumb along the rough ovals of his fingertips, I deduce with all the brilliance of a dirt clod, *This job business is a symptom of deeper trouble.*

"Go home and talk to her," I say, sounding not like a helpful sister but, far worse, a mother. "Let her know how you feel. Tell her the things you've just told me. Okay?"

He leans back in his chair and, I believe, studies me, silently. He is immaculately beautiful. "I have talked to her. It never seems to sink in. But I'll try again."

He kisses me on my cheek as he leaves. He's no sooner

out of my office than I'm muttering to myself about myself, "I am such a fool."

. . .

You CALL ME at work and tell me to meet you at a bar on Fourth Street.

"But you can't drink. The Antabuse, remember?"

"I'm not drinking, Constance. I'm meeting the attorneys there to go over some matters related to the screenplay. Will you be there or won't you?" You are using your playful, authoritarian voice.

"I'll be there around five-thirty."

"Don't be late," you intone, and then you hang up.

. . .

THE PARKING LOT is full. The two-for-one happy hour has packed them in. I find a spot way in the back. In my rearview mirror I powder my face, refresh my lipstick, and run my hand over my hair. I hope the attorneys who are interested in investing in your screenplay have already left. Through no fault of their own they give me the heebie-jeebies. I tell myself to get over it. *I am a professional young working woman. They'd probably give their eyeteeth for me to interview them, and to send Mika out to photograph them at their offices, and for their fat mugs to be spread all over the front page of my paper.* Nice try, but the thought doesn't help. I always feel like a boob around your friends, certain they laugh about us behind our backs.

As I wind my way through this logjam of cars, I spy a dime glinting on the asphalt. I lean over to pick it up, when a sound interlopes from my past, stopping me cold. Someone is moaning, almost growling. It is the same noise my daddy made when he was dying.

I scan the parking lot. Five car lengths away a guy about my age, his tie loose and the underarms of his white oxford shirt stained with sweat, is gawking at something on the ground and is saying, "Holy shit! Are you okay?"

As I approach I see that familiar glint of silver. Audi silver.

Oh dear Jesus, you are having a heart attack. I run. I have to help you. Have to massage your chest and holler at God, like Mama did for Daddy.

The guy is standing over you, seemingly paralyzed. I guess he's scared, too.

"Go get help!" I scream. "Call an ambulance!"

I kneel beside you. You are groaning and your skin is bright red. A stench rises from your pores like heat from asphalt. You have shit on yourself. You are lying in feces and vomit.

"Can you talk?"

"Yeah, yeah, help me up."

"No. Just lie still. They're calling an ambulance."

"No, goddamn it, help me up! It's just the Antabuse. Had a drink."

I try to pull you to your feet. I am unsuccessful. You are too big. You manage to roll over and rise on all fours. You get a grip on your side mirror and pull yourself up and then collapse facedown on the hood.

"Hurry," you say, "get me in the car, get me out of here."

I know how to do this. I listened closely when my mama talked about pulling Daddy out of the bathroom and supporting his weight all the way to their bedroom. There is another reason, too, that I know how to manage this. But I can't think about that right now. You lean on me, and I hurl you toward the passenger side, allowing your weight to propel us. Once in, you toss me the keys.

You vomit into your lap and then yell, "Goddamn it! Get me home!"

.   .   .

I HELP YOU REMOVE your soiled clothes. I prop you up on a chair in the bathroom and start running bathwater. Hot—it's got to be hot, very, very hot. I want your skin sanitized, free of any hint of shit. But first, I gather your clothes and put them in a trash bag. We must get rid of the evidence. The reminders. The annoying memories.

The worst of the Antabuse reaction seems to be over, but you are still red-hot and reeking.

"Let's get you in the tub."

"No! I don't want to lay in it."

Of course not. What was I thinking? I flip the faucet knob

onto the shower setting. I test the water temperature. I help you in. You lean against the shower wall. I fear you will fall. I fear I will not be able to catch you. I soap up a washcloth and begin cleaning the shit from your thighs. I work my way up. I know how to do this. I am a good daughter . . .

. . .

IT IS 1977 and I'm a college freshman at University of Tampa. I have a full academic scholarship which I'm real proud of. I didn't apply to any other schools. Most of my high school friends left home for college. University of Florida. Florida State. Emory. But not me. Mama says she needs me. Mama says she can't get on without me. My brother lives in Texas and my sister is married. So it's just me and Mama, now.

I have never learned to drive—Mama won't allow it—so right before school started we moved into a tenement apartment building located directly across the street from UT. It's got air conditioning. That's a first for us.

The apartment building is named The Spartan Arms. That's because of the University of Tampa Spartans. But I've dubbed the place The Tarantula Arms in homage to Blanche DuBois's old haunt.

It's full of crackpots. Some of them are dangerous, I'm sure. For instance, we're positive that the guy in 316 is on the run from the law, but we can't figure out what for. Mama says she's going to ask him. She says we have a right to know. I hope it's not murder. Also, there are a few people on probation. You can tell them a mile away. They seem to live mysterious half-lives, as if by staying away from the rest of us they might not be inclined to resume their criminal ways. One of the artists who lives on the floor above us says their crimes read like a laundry list of hopelessness (his phrase, not mine): petty theft, grand larceny, tax evasion, drug dealing, drug addiction, and, yeah, murder.

Winos sleep in the lobby. They use the stairwell and elevator as their bathroom. I hate going in and out of the building. I'm afraid they might rape me or something. This is a shameful way to think. I know Scripture. I became real religious a few years ago. Jesus would make these guys his friends. One or two might become disciples. I guess I'm just not Christian enough. Maybe it would be different if I was a man. Then the sex part wouldn't be an issue.

Like I said, this place is a revolving door. Tenants come. Tenants go. But there are some people who really live here, for whom The Tarantula Arms is home in the sense that they don't plan to move anytime soon. Some are drifters who've gotten too old to drift. Others, like the two artists upstairs, stay because it's cheap, and they believe they are living Bohemian lives.

The artists have sort of taken me under their wings and have taught me to smoke marijuana (but I don't do that very often, as I still think it might be a sin; they counter that no,

Jesus smoked weed, but I wonder how they know that since they are Jewish), and to appreciate jazz, and to sharpen my debating skills.

Then there are the Scientologists who sell cures in little glass vials filled with colorless fluids. Mysterious concoctions that act as panaceas for body and soul.

We live on the third floor in a one-bedroom apartment that has a decent view of the street which the rest of the city has dubbed Derelict Row.

Mama misses digging in dirt. Potting soil, she says, is beyond our means so she grows plants in water-filled wine bottles. Their root systems flourish, suspended in a strange and wild tangle, fed by water and light.

She sleeps on the couch in the living room. This isn't anything to feel real sorry for her about, not because it isn't sad but because she is used to it. It is her choice. She has refused to sleep in a real bed since the night Daddy died. That was a long time ago.

I am in my room, which I have fancifully decided to think of as a monastic cell. I have no furniture other than the mattress, no window, no bric-a-brac to suggest small joys. My faux-ivory plastic crucifix with the gold-tone corpus hangs above my bed. The sole indulgence in this room is books. They are everywhere. Stacks lean into one another. In some cases, they serve as impromptu furniture. My bed is my desk. It is where I study, which is what I'm doing now.

Mama calls to me from the living room. She says, "Jesus Christ, he's killing the man! Connie, get in here!"

I don't believe her. She exaggerates all the time. Like when she doesn't want me to do something, such as go on a trip with my friends or study for a semester in Europe on a complete scholarship, she claims she has cancer. *Liar, liar, pants on fire,* that's what I think.

But I'd better do what she says. I don't want to get slapped. Or beaten with that brush again. So I push aside my papers and head into the living room. This is actually not a bad room. It has a bank of tall windows which look out over the street. They allow in lots of natural light which her plants seem to love. Mama stands at the central window, hands on her wide hips, a cigarette lodged between arthritis-domed knuckles.

"Jesus!" she repeats, her voice shaking.

"What's up?"

She seems unable to pull her gaze away from whatever is happening on the street. "Why doesn't somebody do something?"

I join her at the window. I look at the street three floors below. Dear Jesus, she isn't making this one up. On the sidewalk across the street in front of the church, one man has another by the ankles and is pounding his head into the pavement. It's as if he's using the man as a human jackhammer. I give in to that horrible human tendency to be so repulsed I can't look away. It's as if curiosity comes with a scorpion's tail. Insanely, I wonder where the attacker gets his strength. I mean, this can't be easy. He lifts the man's entire body up and down, up and down with rapid-fire jamming motions.

The victim is unconscious. His face, blood covered, appears frozen in a caricatured expression of surprised pain. On the upswing his head dangles as if it is no longer connected by bone to the rest of his body. It swings crazily, like the unhinged head of a jack-in-the-box.

I turn away. "Mama, don't look."

She glares as if I've just cursed at her and then starts slapping my arms. She isn't hitting hard, simply frenetically. I let her. I've learned to never fight back. I just stand there, going inside myself, to my blank white space. No emotion exists there.

Soon enough, just as I predicted, she quits hitting and refocuses her attention on the murder. I can't help it, I look, too.

A couple of guys who appear to be construction workers dash from our side of the street to that of the assailant's. It takes their combined strength but they manage to pull the attacker's hands off his victim's ankles. The dead man falls heavily, the proverbial sack of potatoes, onto the sidewalk. It looks as if the construction workers are caught off guard by the sprawling body because they momentarily freeze, gapemouthed, giving the attacker all the time he needs to escape. No one gives chase. They kneel beside the body as if their concern might render a resurrection. I bet they don't even know him. I bet they're simply being good Samaritans. I should feel honored to be in their presence.

Mama fists her trembling hand and brings it to her mouth.

"Oh! Goddamn son of a bitch!" she says through gritted teeth.

She falls onto the couch and stares hopelessly into the air. Her hair has fallen into her eyes, and her entire body slumps into the couch as if her life force has been sucked away by witnessing a stranger's murder.

I don't know what to do. A man is dead. I can't help him. I can't help Mama. My stomach cramps. I am sickened by my own inefficacy. Maybe I should pray.

"Why? Why?"

"I don't know, Mama. Try not to think about it."

She looks at me as if I'm her only hope in all the world. And suddenly I know what's coming.

"Go down to the corner and get me a bottle. There's money in my purse."

I hate doing this. Hate going to the corner. Even the frat boys avoid that place. It's a wino store. The drunks waver among the bottles—stinking, spectral, hollow-eyed—as if they are the walking dead. I am eighteen years old. Never tasted liquor—Mama doesn't allow it. She says she can't go. Not after seeing that. So I've got to do it. She's gotta have a drink. It's the only thing that will calm her nerves. Don't I understand? Or am I too high and mighty to walk down there and get her a harmless little bottle?

"What about the murderer? He's out there somewhere."

"You think he's gonna bother with somebody like you! Give me a break!"

Then she calls me some names which I block out by humming inside my head "On the Wings of a Snow White Dove."

Then I do as I'm told. I get the money from her purse. I walk down the mildew-stinking hall to the piss-stinking elevator (I avoid the stairwell in case the killer is hiding in there—I've seen those movies) and out into the hard light of day, where a man lies dead. I am dizzy. Maybe fear is making me dizzy. No, it's probably just the heat. I walk right past the dead man, who is now shielded by a ring of gawking bums. I pause long enough to look up at our apartment. Mama is back at the window, hovering over the scene below like a bloated old crow. I continue on, giving wide berth to a drunk who is passed out before noon—halfway in the gutter, the other half on the sidewalk—a spent bottle of Thunderbird resting in his palm.

I am very close now. All I have to do is cross a two-lane street and I'm there. But I am afraid of the corner store. Afraid that a derelict might get fresh with me. Afraid he might rape me, knowing the way bad men do that I'm a virgin (Mama was raped on a street corner, why isn't she scared that I might suffer the same fate?). Afraid of the disgusting odor of an unwashed, fetid human. Afraid that the store will be robbed while I'm in it (robbery is a frequent occurrence, people looking for quick drug money, that's what people in our building say). Afraid of running into the killer. Afraid that someone I go to school with will see me. Afraid that President Cheshire, himself, will drive by right as I reach for the door. Goddamn it! I push it open and step inside.

The store is about the size of a decent closet. It specializes in Thunderbird and Three Roses and Midnight Train and Colt 45 Malt Liquor. A derelict who smells of his own urine and shit stands maybe three feet away from me, coughing so hard he doubles over. His sputum rains down and congeals on the vinyl floor. I approach the counter, thinking this is just like the nightmare when I'm being chased by a snake and my legs turn to rubber and I fall down and I can't move no matter how hard I try, even though I know the snake is closing in.

"Early Times, please."

"Pint or quart?" asks the old Cuban man who works days.

I shrug my shoulders. "Whatever's cheaper."

That night, amid sirens and honking horns and the general din of traffic, Mama goes on a crying jag. It's just like the ones from the old days in the trailer except now they last longer. And back then, bewildered and nonsensical hope prevented her sadness from consuming her bone by bone. But no more. Here she is, a woman in her mid-fifties, carrying the baggage of rape and spousal abuse and poverty, and she no longer has the time, the patience, the youth to kid herself into believing that tomorrow will be a better day. She does not have good days. They are all behind her.

We do the dance.

Hold me, Connie. Come over here and hold me. I need to be

held. *I love you. I love you so much. I gave up everything for you girls. I've sacrificed day and night. I wish God would strike me dead right this second. No, please, Connie, don't go! Don't ever leave me. You're all I've got.*

I'm all she's got, all she's got, all she's got, all she's got . . .

"It's okay, Mama. I'm not gonna leave you. I promise."

I wet a washcloth and put it to her face. She pushes me away. It is four o'clock in the morning. I have an 8:00 A.M. class. If I don't keep up my grades, I will lose my scholarship. But I can't leave her. I can't be a bad daughter. Somehow, that would be a double sin. A sin on God and a sin on Mama.

"Mama, why don't you try to sleep some?"

She mumbles. I don't understand. She pours herself a drink. She picks up her pack of Vantage which she says is better for her than the Salems. It's empty. She crushes it and says, "Get me that other pack."

"Where is it?"

"I don't know. Just find it!"

She stays on the couch, sitting upright, the white sheet bunched up around her crotch, mumbling, ruminating, drinking, holding court over her trusty pint of Early Times. The ashtray is overflowing with stubs. But I will not clean it. That's where I draw the line. And it's a perfect line because she doesn't know it exists.

I tear up the apartment looking for the cigarettes. Kitchen cupboards. Kitchen drawers. Her purse. The bookcase. My bedroom. The windowsills. The bathroom. We have no cigarettes.

"Mama, I can't find them."

She looks at me. She works her lips in and out, and her eyes begin to madly dart. She explodes.

"You are so goddamned helpless. You make me sick! You stupid, lousy bitch!"

She reaches for a stub and lights it.

"I'm going to bed now, Mama."

In seconds, her face flashes from anger to disgust to hurt. She bursts into tears. Again.

"Oh, Connie. Please. Please don't do this to me. I can't go on like this."

She offers me her hand. "Please?"

I want to strike her. I want to yell, "Leave me alone!" and, "Why don't you just die!"

But, of course, I do not. I am a good daughter, no matter what she says. I take her hand.

She pulls me down beside her. She clings to me. Her sweat is on my skin. She sobs and mumbles and curses and pleads. Each time I try to leave, her hysteria flares. She is a wildfire. Out of control. There's nothing I can do. Nothing at all. There is nothing new about any of this. We've done it all before. So many times. This is the dance.

We do not stop until dawn. As night gives way to the faltering glow of a new morning, exhaustion finally wins out and she falls heavily asleep.

I wash my face, gather my books, and wander across the street where we will discuss nineteenth-century British Romantic poetry.

.　.　.

YOUR SHIT IS under my nails and in my hair.

I decide I cannot do this. I won't do this.

You cuss into air made thick with steam. Your skin is no longer red from the Antabuse reaction but from the fury with which I've scrubbed.

I hate you. I hate your sickness. I hate me. I hate the memories that won't ebb. . . .

.　.　.

I THINK THAT watching that man get murdered was a bad thing.

Mama, she's not doing well. She's sick but nobody believes me. Maybe it's the buckteeth, I don't know, but when I say I think we need to get her some help, people look at me as if I've lost my mind. This is what I think. I think that when we watched a man being murdered from our perch on the third floor, we invited in death, giving it a new place to roost and fester.

For instance, Mama's physical appearance is startling. Her belly is distended. Her skull seems to be shrinking back in on itself, causing her eyes to appear as if they are bulging out of her head. And the whites have taken on a yellow cast (she blames this on the vitamin C which she started taking in massive doses on the recommendation of the Scientologists). Her skin is clammy. She smells like rot. The silver in her hair no longer shimmers in the light. It's yellow, too. Shampooing doesn't help.

One of the Scientologists has a friend who purports to be an expert in homeopathy. He deals in small glass vials filled with clear fluids which, he claims, are infused with special healing herbs.

Mama drinks the potions with abandon. I guess I have to hand it to the snake oil homeopathist. She does seem happier. She says the concoctions make her feel a hundred times better.

Her hands have become speckled with dark freckles. The homeopathist diagnoses them as youth spots. Her body, he claims, is rejuvenating itself.

Still, I have doubts. Perhaps my cynicism is the result of my education. I beg her to go to a real doctor. She tells me I'm a fool. I call up my sister and ask for help.

"Maybe if you make the appointment and take her there, so she doesn't have to drive?"

"We can't force her to get help."

"Will you at least talk to her?"

Deidre calls her several times but to no avail. Every time either of us broaches the subject Mama lashes out.

I decide Deidre is right. We can't force her.

One morning, just past daybreak, a noxious odor hustles

me from my sleep. I think that maybe our toilet has backed up. I get out of bed and stumble into the bathroom. The plumbing seems to be in working order. I walk into the living room, holding my nose. The stench makes me gag. I approach the couch on tiptoe, but I'm too late. Mama is awake and lying in shit.

"I'm sorry," she says. "You're gonna have to clean it up."

I don't think about it. I just do it. I go to the white space.

Mama outweighs me two times over, so getting her off the couch is not an easy chore. But I remember her helping Daddy. She told her friends she used superhuman power, that God helped her, that she'd learned how to hoist deadweight back when she was a nursing student.

I try to pull her up by her arms, but she yells that it hurts and slaps me away. She hasn't any strength in her lower body, so I have to figure out a way to do the work for her. I put my arms around her chest and tug as hard as I can. I try one, two, three times. The stench seems to be alive. It is growing. Blooming. White space. White space. Return to the white space. I do and it works. On the fourth go, I get her to her feet. I groan under the weight and stumble backward, but manage not to lose her.

She is silent. We are locked together, face-to-face, equally determined. We know what we must do. We must traverse the five feet between the couch and the bathroom. I get us aimed in the right direction and then sort of hurl us forward, propelled by her deadweight. My head hits the doorjamb.

"Goddamn it!" I yell, not pausing to apologize for cussing in front of her, not even apologizing to God. I get a good grip on the wall, and I use it to steady us as we make the final lurch into the bathroom.

I know I can't get her into the tub without doing serious damage to at least one of us, so I prop her on the toilet and pause to catch my breath. Then I undress her. She doesn't look at me, which I think is best for both of us. Maybe she has a white space of her own. I run scalding hot tap water and soap up the washcloth. I scrub the hardened shit off of her ass and legs. I try to be gentle but it's impossible. Dried excrement is tantamount to a bonding agent. What I need is a chisel, not a washrag. I do not attempt to make conversation. There's no way to soft sell this. So I just keep scrubbing and rinsing and soaping. Scrubbing and rinsing and soaping. Scrubbing and rinsing and soaping, my hands touching parts of my mama's body that I never wanted to see.

Her skin is thin, nearly translucent, and yellow, like the faint edge of a bruise. Scattered throughout the yellow flesh are spider veins—thin and endless, a gathering of thorns.

When I'm done, I toss the washrag in the trash and ask, "Do you need to go again?"

She nods and continues to stare at a fixed spot on the wall.

I pick up her nightgown (it is ruined) and leave the room, closing the door behind me. I quickly gather up the soiled sheets and she yells, "Leave them alone. I'll get them!"

She can't get them. We both know that. She can't even walk. But I find her attempt to save face endearing. This shocks me. I haven't found anything endearing about her since I was five. Quickly, I stuff the soiled sheets and gown into a garbage bag and set them by the door.

When I hear her flush, I tap on the door and say, "I've got some clean clothes for you."

"Big deal!" she says, that old sarcasm thick as ever.

I step inside and hand them to her. She manages to pull the shell over her head and the shorts up to her thighs. To finish the job, I'll have to get her on her feet.

She looks at me. "Well? You just gonna stand there?"

Again, I try pulling her to her feet. I try five times. She is getting angrier. I decide I can't do it. Whatever freakish strength allowed me to get her into the bathroom is gone.

"I have to go get help."

"No!" Her voice is thick and, I think, fed by shame.

So I try again. This has to work. We have no choice. My arms and legs shake. My spine feels as if it might snap. I close my eyes and grunt.

Somehow, she rises to her feet. Once she's up, she holds on to the towel rack while I pull up her underwear and shorts. We bump and fumble, attempting to figure out the best way to get her back to the couch. I figure I need to face forward so I can at least see where I'm trying to go. She agrees and drapes herself against my back.

Like a hunter bringing home a carcass, I half-carry, half-drag Mama into the living room.

. . .

You HAVE SURVIVED the Antabuse. You leaned on me—a gigantic, helpless, naked, freshly scrubbed child—as I guided us out of the bathroom and into our bedroom. You are there now, under the white sheet, snoring.

As I watch you sleep I wonder, Why didn't the Antabuse kill you? Why hasn't the drinking killed you? Or the smoking? No one is supposed to engage so freely in self-abuse and live.

You are totally relaxed. Slack-jawed. Legs and arms akimbo. Not a stitch of a nightmare. Just blessed repose.

You know what I think? You are dying. And I am watching. A handmaid to your death.

For the first time in my life, I know the future. As with Mama, there will be more treks to the bathroom. More scrubbing the excrement off your skin. Clothes and sheets to throw away because you have shit in them. Sleepless nights during which I hold cold compresses to your head to ease your fever. Wretched hours spent trying to cajole you into eating a bowl of toast soaked in warm milk, but you will push away the food and order me to pour you another drink.

And you will never thank me. You will be too angry.

. . .

I STEP INTO Mama's hospital room.

Deidre is there, sitting in a chair beside the bed, her

hands folded on her lap, her posture stiff and erect. She is holding a death vigil. In fact, for five days now, she has sat nearly motionless, bearing witness to the final hours of Mama's life.

I do not have the wherewithal or courage to join this vigil for more than a few hours a day. Oddly enough, I bear no guilt over this. Somehow, the six years I spent living alone with Mama, carrying the full weight of her madness, has allowed me this freedom.

But poor Deidre, she has no such freedom. In an act of sacrificial masochism, she is taking in all of this, fully giving herself over to the tragedy, keeping no part of her soul untouched. And I fear for her.

Almost every second of every day she sits and stares. She talks to nurses and doctors and nuns. She eases Mama's aching skin with hand lotion. She holds glasses of fruit juice just so, enabling Mama to suck nourishment through a straw. She listens to Mama's wild ramblings, her devout curses, her whispered regrets. Just yesterday, Mama told her that she thinks this time she really screwed up, that she waited too long to get help. Deidre had to lean in close to hear these words. I hope Deidre throws them away. Everything uttered in this room needs to be erased from her memory bank so that they will not stalk her days, weeks, years down the line.

Mama is asleep. At least her eyes are closed. I walk over to Deidre and she flashes a faint, exhausted smile. Her face is gaunt. Her eyes are red and swollen from tears. But I don't mention the tears because we both know that what she is crying about doesn't have anything to do with Mama dying. It's all about being unable to make sense of what this woman has done. To us. And to herself.

"How is she?"

"The same."

I put my hand on Deidre's shoulder and together we stare at Mama's bloated yellow body cocooned within clean white sheets. Tubes snake in and out of her. Monitors hum steadily as if they are alive and breathing.

"Why don't you go get a cup of coffee?"

"You sure?"

"Yes. Go. You need a break."

Deidre rises unsteadily to her feet. She leaves the room, clutching her shoulder bag tight against her body.

I stare down at my mama. I try not to be frightened by the tubes and their slow-moving fluids. But I am. She opens her eyes and, startled, I jump back.

"Hi, Mama," I say.

She doesn't speak, but simply lies there, staring at the ceiling, the whites of her eyes stained saffron.

On the bus ride over here, I decided my goal on this visit was to be uplifting. An angel of mercy. I've heard that sometimes when people are sick, small talk is helpful. So now that Mama is awake, I try to implement my plan. I try to tell Mama about my day.

"I got a good grade on that essay I've been working on. And oh, Miss Lewis, the lady in 412, is moving out, but I don't know where to. I asked permission to leave my lit class early so I could catch the two-fifteen bus and Dr. Solomon, my English professor, said to tell you he's thinking about you and hopes you're well very soon."

That is all I say, I swear to God, but the second the words are out of my mouth, her yellow eyes ignite. I pull back even though I know she can't hit me. She is connected to too many tubes to be able to rise from the bed and slap, or kick, or punch, or strangle.

But her illness has not dampened her rage. And it is her rage that I fear, have always feared. She doesn't move her head in my direction. Only her bulging yellow eyes. I am fully in her sights when she spits, "Tell him to go to hell. *You* go to hell."

I don't know what to do. I want to fly away, back into my white space. But she has landed a solid blow. Shattered the white space all to hell.

And suddenly I know what the white space has always done for me. It has protected me from the truth: My mama hates me.

Oh my God, no. I stand here, in the antiseptic cube of a hospital room, hanging on to the cold steel rails of her bed, blinking back tears, telling myself she doesn't mean it.

It's the drugs talking. Just the drugs. She doesn't know what she's saying.

But deep down, in the place inside all of us where scars rot and smolder and never heal, I know otherwise.

So I don't talk anymore and neither does Mama. I listen

to the machines. They have a steady rhythm. *You go to hell. You go to hell. You go to hell.*

When Deidre returns, I whisper, "I have to leave now, or else I'll miss the last bus home."

"Phil can take you."

I shake my head. I can't risk any words right now. Don't trust myself. Don't know what I might do if I don't get out of here.

Maybe there is time left for me to still be a good daughter.

I bend over and kiss Mama good-bye.

She flinches at my touch.

.   .   .

BACK AT THE apartment, I think about dying. We have a gas stove. Easy enough. That's what Sylvia Plath did. And I like her. Everyone does. She is famous. Dying made her famous.

In the wake of my death, my poetry professor might collect all my poems into a chapbook that becomes a bestseller and causes people everywhere to cry and to reflect, "She was a decent person. It's a damn shame, what happened to her."

I walk into our cubbyhole kitchen. I open the oven door. I'm not sure of the mechanics. I guess you just turn on the gas and stick in your head. So that's what I do. I set the oven to three-fifty. If it's good enough for a casserole, it ought to be good enough for me. I try to get my head all the way into the core of the oven, but my body isn't long enough. Neither is my neck.

How did Sylvia manage? Maybe she was blessed with one of those long slender necks that caused people to comment on her pure and effortless sophistication. An Audrey Hepburn neck.

I'm realizing now that when Dr. Locke lectured about her suicide, he left out some really important details. I guess I'll just have to settle for draping myself over the oven door.

The meatloaf splatter is sticky against my cheek. I bet they put that part in the paper. *When found, her face was scarred with meatloaf splatter.*

I sure hope the gas gets to me before the heat does. I don't want to burn. Just gas myself. Just go to sleep and not wake up. I tell myself to relax. But it's not easy. My knees are starting to hurt. And the top of my head is getting awfully hot. Fuck it. Sylvia must have been a hell of a woman. I get up and turn off the oven.

Then I scrub my face. The meatloaf splatter clings like snot. It sort of makes me sick, so I scrub so hard my skin hurts. But being clean makes me feel a little bit better. Maybe that's what I need to do—clean this joint from top to bottom. Yes. The woodwork, the floors, the windows, everything. Get rid of Mama's scent. I'll even mop under and behind our furniture. I'll start with that couch. That goddamn couch. If Mama lives—maybe even if she doesn't—I'm throwing that motherfucker out.

I change into cutoffs and an old tee. I tie a bandana

around my head to keep the hair out of my eyes. I march into the living room. I devise a plan. Pull the couch away from the wall. Sweep behind it. Clear out all the dust. Then mop. And mop. And mop. The whole place.

First I move the coffee table out of the way. Then I crouch like a wrestler and stick both hands under the bottom rail of the couch. I establish a really firm grip, and I pull. Hard. I want a good two-to-three-foot clearance between the couch and wall. But wait a minute. I don't understand. What is all this clinking? Breaking? Shattering? Rolling? Cascading? Forever. On and on. Like the surf. The sound we fled from. The sound that was forbidden simply through the circumstances of our exile. *"Once we leave this place, we'll never hear the surf again."* But these are not waves crashing onto the shore. They are empty booze bottles that Mama secretly stashed behind the couch. So many bottles. Hundreds of them. Falling and falling, sometimes breaking, until the floor is covered.

This is so bad. So really, really bad. She must have lain on the couch drinking herself into oblivion, too loaded to do anything other than throw the empties behind her.

How long has she been doing this? For years? Or just a few weeks? Maybe this was her suicide attempt.

How could I be so stupid? Why didn't I know? I am culpable. This is my fault. All my fault. All my fault.

I put my hands to my temples and grit my teeth and scream. I could jab the broken end of a bottle into my jugular. Or slit my throat from ear to ear. Mama has threatened to do that, herself. I would bleed to death fast. It probably wouldn't even hurt all that bad.

But that's not the point, is it? What good is my suicide if I don't suffer? The point is, I must be punished. I have to stay alive so that I get what is due me. Death is too easy. If I stay alive, I know that eventually my punishment will come.

So this is it. This is how it goes. I clean up the bottles. I put them in garbage bags. I sweep the floor. I get out the flashlight and search for any stray slivers of glass. I find lots.

I fill five garbage bags. I will sneak them out of the building, one by one, over the course of the next few days under the cover of night. I don't want anyone to know. I must protect Mama, keep her reputation pristine. I heat a can of lima beans and eat a bowlful, surrounded by the booze bottle–filled bags. I feel sort of okay, like I have a mission. Protect Mama. I'm comfortable with that.

When I'm done with my bowl of beans, I leave the apartment, a single bag in hand. I run into Ira, one of the artists, in the hall.

"What are you doing?"

"Cleaning."

"How's your mom?"

"Fine."

"I'll take that for you."

"No!"

"Well, why don't I just walk with you then?"

"No, I've got it. I don't need any help."

"You know that homeopathist who's been running around here? I found out what's in his little glass tubes."

"What?"

"Rubbing alcohol. One hundred percent pure."

"Ah, Jesus!"

"When you're done, why don't you come up? I've made some brownies."

"No, I've really got to study."

"Are you okay?"

"I'm absolutely fine. See ya', Ira."

And I duck into the stairwell, not caring if a wino rapes me, damning myself because the bottles keep clinking.

I throw the bag in the Dumpster behind Plant Hall. It's late. Nobody is around. Nobody sees me.

When I get home I try to sleep, but those hate words keep playing in my mind. It sure is a stuck record.

You *go to hell*. You *go to hell*. You *go to hell*.

At 5:00 A.M. the phone rings. I know who it is. I pick it up.

"Hi."

"They just called. She died about twenty minutes ago. I'm going over there now. They say I have to sign some papers. Will you be there?"

Deidre is on automatic. I understand. It's the white space. *A, B, C.* Dot, dot, dot.

"Yeah. Sure. I'll find a ride." I hang up the phone.

The punishment has begun. I am in free-fall. The woman

whom I loved more than anyone on the planet, the woman who gave birth to me, the woman whom I fantasized killing, the woman whose last words to me were, *"You* go to hell," is dead.

And I suddenly know that I do not have a clue how to walk out that door and function in the world without her.

. . .

CHILDREN LOVE THEIR PARENTS. It's a natural law. When we're babies they bathe us and feed us and tickle our bellies and say, "Coo-cootchy-coo."

I don't think we ever forget that.

. . .

DEIDRE, Jimmy, and I all love her. She is our soul. When she hollered or hit or hurled epithets, it only strengthened our resolve to be better children.

Yes, each of us lived and breathed for one solitary purpose: to try and please her.

And we failed.

. . .

YOU HAVE THREE MORE close calls with the Antabuse before I decide enough is enough. I find your stash and flush it down the toilet. I'm not going to clean up your shit anymore.

．　．　．

Something inside me has changed. I'm getting hard. Bitter, maybe. I don't feel as sorry for you as I once did.

I come home late, around ten o'clock, after having dinner with Heather and George.

You are drunk and raging. You scream the same old tune. They are out to use me. They are nothing but a couple of creeps, crooks, cunts—your words.

You're not making sense. And I know it. For the first time, I know it.

．　．　．

I am at work, editing stories for the next issue. No one in the office suspects anything. They do not know that last night you tried to rape me with a booze bottle. I will tell no one. They will never know that I managed to run out of the house, grabbing my keys off the desk in the sunroom. They will never know that Katie started barking and ran with me down the porch stairs. They will never know that if I'm a bit red-eyed, it's because Katie and I drove around downtown St. Pete until 4:00 A.M. They will never know that when we returned you were passed out on the couch, and that we snuck back in through the porch and barricaded ourselves in the bedroom.

．　．　．

MIKA STOPS BY the office around three. I am thrilled. And I tell myself to stop it. The last thing I need is a lover. I might not be the most experienced gal in town, but even I know that sex can ruin an otherwise decent relationship. Besides, Mika is just being nice. Why on earth would he want to be intimate with a bucktoothed broad?

I fix us a fresh pot of coffee. We sit in my office.

He says, "You look tired."

I pick at a frayed thread on my blouse sleeve. "I didn't get much sleep last night."

"I'm sorry. Is everything all right?"

"Oh yeah. Everything is fine. How have you been?"

"Good. I've been working on a new series of photographs. Black-and-white nude portraiture. I'm trying some different things. I don't know if they're any good or not."

"I bet they're wonderful. I'd love to see them sometime."

"Really?"

"Yes, really."

He says it surprises him whenever anyone shows interest in his art.

"I understand," I say. "It's like my poetry. No one cares about it but me. And that's okay. Because I'm not writing it for anyone else."

"I would love to read your work."

He stares at me with that steady gaze of his, and I feel like I'm drowning. But in a good way.

And I also think that all this talk about photography and

poetry is really about something deeper, but then I stop myself because that is a dangerous thought.

.   .   .

I AM SO GRATEFUL that you are not home. If I'm lucky, you'll
be gone for days. I feed the dogs. God muscles Katie away
from her bowl. As always, she capitulates. I can't stand it. I
take Katie and her food to the front porch and close the door
so that she can eat in peace. Then she and I go for a walk.
When we return, I heat a can of soup. I'm going through the
motions of a life, but I feel completely disconnected. I am
becoming invisible.

With both dogs following me, I wander into the sunroom
and sit at the desk. Then, I defy you. I use your typewriter.

I make a list. I title it "What I Am." I love the sound of the
keys against the page.

> *Editor*
>
> *Writer (poetry, stories, song lyrics, grocery,
> and to-do lists)*
>
> *Journalist*
>
> *Cook*
>
> *Former championship baton twirler*
>
> *Jogger*

Mother to Kateland

Good thrift-store shopper

Ugly

In need of a new face

Smart?

Independent?

I erase the last two. I remove the page from the typewriter and slip it into my briefcase. I close my eyes. I concentrate really hard: *Find a way to change your life.*

.   .   .

You breeze in at around nine-thirty, reeking of cigarettes and beer. I'm sitting on the couch, reading. Katie is curled beside me, and God is asleep by my feet. You don't acknowledge us. Instead you head straight for the bathroom. I hear you throw up. I cover my ears with my hands. After a few minutes, I hear the faucet running and you gargling.

A month ago I would have stood outside the door, asking if I could help you. But not now.

.   .   .

You walk into the living room, wiping your face with a towel.

I look at you. Why am I unafraid? "You okay?"

You don't answer. You go into the kitchen. I hear you pour yourself a drink. You come back in with a glass of whiskey. You sit down in the chair across from me. "You know, kiddo, why don't you ever clean that fucking thing out?"

"What fucking thing?"

"The fucking thing between your legs. It's like a cesspool in there. It makes me puke."

And just like that, my nerve, my meanness, my fledgling self-respect is shot all to hell. "I'm sorry," I say. "I'm really, really sorry."

. . .

YOU HAVE FALLEN ASLEEP. The TV is still on. Some old movie. I'm not interested. But the flickering glow of the screen prevents the bedroom from being totally dark.

As I drift toward sleep, I hang on tight to Katie and I have this thought: *The next time Mika stops by the office, I will remove from my top desk drawer my chapbook of poems, which were published by University of Tampa Press when I was a sophomore, and I will photocopy them for him. I will fold the pages in half and hand them to him. I will not tell him what they are. I will not beg him to read them.*

Instead, I will say without flourish, "Here, these are for you. I think maybe you will understand."

. . .

KATIE HAS BEEN escaping on a regular basis. She doesn't run away. She stands in the front yard, barking, wagging her tail, smiling sheepishly when I come out to get her.

You say that one of the dogs moves the concrete blocks I put there to prevent them from wiggling out between the stair runners. I say, "That's not possible." And you say, "Then how come I have to keep putting them back?"

.   .   .

IT'S SATURDAY MORNING. You're sleeping late. The ugly, angry part of me hopes you never wake.

I put Katie and God in the run after I feed them, and then stand quietly at the window and watch. For a while they both engage in typical dog stuff. Pooping. Peeing. Sniffing. God tries to nudge and paw Katie into a game. Katie snaps. She's not in any mood. God takes it in stride. Katie walks over to the stairs. She looks at God as if to say, "Hey, get over here." And he does. She sniffs at the concrete blocks. She pushes her face against God's and then sniffs the blocks again. This time God figures it out. He begins digging around the blocks and manages to dislodge them. As soon as there is a sufficiently large opening, Katie zips through. And God just stands there, looking confused, wagging his tail.

I think, *Wow, Katie sure is talented!* And, *What a smart dog I have!* I meet her at the front door. I kneel down and hug her. She licks my face.

"What a good escape artist you are! Such a good girl!"

· · ·

I'm sitting in Heather and George's living room. It's a comfortable space, filled with cats, books, plants, art, and Heather's piano.

Heather and I are drinking wine and eating cheese. This makes me feel grown-up. Which is a good thing. But as I nibble on a cracker, I also admit to myself that I'm ashamed. Because even though Heather and I are having a perfectly lovely time, what I'm really hoping for is that out of sheer luck Mika will stop by. I would take this as a sign from God that maybe my romantic interest in him is not a sin. Sometimes I think that what is truly wrong with me is that I can't control my heart. I mean, I'm in enough trouble all on my own. Why would I complicate things further by getting involved with a married man? And what if my instincts are totally unreliable? What if he's not good and decent, but just another guy out to boff anything in a skirt? That's what Mama said all men are out for. That none of them are decent.

I reach for my wine glass. I feel a need to confess. Heather brings this out in me. I can confide in her. "I'm hiding money. Every week since I started at the magazine I've put a little aside that he doesn't know about. I'm going to use it to get my teeth fixed."

Heather doesn't appear to be shocked by my transgression. I'm positive that there are people in this world who would tell me that I'm going straight to hell because, if you think about it, this kind of secret is basically a lie.

But Heather proves to have a very progressive attitude toward sin.

"If this is something you really want to do, then go for it. George and I will support you all the way." And then she says with quiet, unchallengeable authority that the doctor I saw when I was fourteen didn't know what he was talking about.

"Yes," I agree, "he was an asshole. I hope his dick has fallen off."

I don't laugh and neither does she. She just nods as if dicks fall off every day, and it's something assholes should expect.

She then tells me about Mika's wife. She doesn't do it in a mean fashion. Heather hasn't a mean bone in her body. She's a vegetarian. She just explains without rancor that in her opinion Mika would be much better off if he got a divorce. And it's not about Pus Head's (that's my private nickname for The Wife) refusal to work. It's about her controlling him.

Heather confides that The Wife doesn't like any of Mika's friends. In fact, he invited Heather and George over to dinner so they could all meet and start a cozy friendship between couples. Like in the movies. But the cozy friendship never happened because, in the middle of what was shaping up to be an okay evening, Pus Head stomped out of the kitchen and into the living room and screamed at Heather and George, blaming them for everything from Mika's bad attitude to third-world debt to the rise of the far right.

Personally, I don't think anyone should scream at

Heather and George. They're so good they won't even kill ants that crawl across their counter. They take them outside into the fresh air and say, "Have a good life!"

·   ·   ·

MIKA AND I have to go to Miami together. We are doing a story about a man who invents safety equipment for the space shuttle. This is strictly a business trip. No romance. No sin. No mistakes.

You are not happy about this turn of affairs. Yet your discontent does not rattle me. In a stern internal monologue, I remind myself that I'm a journalist. I have a story to write. This is my job.

"The publisher wants the interview done in person. And Mr. Rush is the cover story so Mika has to go."

"If he lays one hand on you, I'll break every bone in his scrawny body."

"Mr. Rush isn't scrawny," I quip, trying to keep things light. I grab Katie's leash off the kitchen table and snap it onto her collar. "Let's go for a walk, little girl."

As we head out the door you yell, "You're not fooling me!"

In my head I yell, *Yes I am!*

·   ·   ·

WHEN KATIE AND I return from our walk, you are gone. Good riddance!

I go into the bathroom and brush my teeth. With my mouth full of toothpaste foam, I smile at my reflection.

Maybe my overbite isn't as bad as I think.

Maybe if I become a successful person, my looks won't matter.

No, that doesn't make sense.

Try this. Maybe if I become a successful person, I will get my teeth fixed, and then I'll go to New Delhi and work for Mother Theresa, and no one will be able to say I ran away be-cause I was ugly.

. . .

PREDAWN, Mika picks me up at my house. We are catching the red-eye out of Tampa and will return from Miami shortly after midnight.

This should all be very simple, but it's not. The ins and outs of transportation have been complicated by our separate domestic situations.

The plan is for Mika to leave his car at the airport, and then Pus Head will have a friend drive her over to pick it up. She needs the car. Why is a mystery, since people claim she does nothing but sit at home and watch soaps. Maybe Mika is not leveling with me. I don't know. I cannot know. I don't need to know. I am not a player in their relationship.

As for me driving my car, I can't. You won't allow it. Three days ago, in a sudden and uncharacteristic concern for my well-being, you insisted, "You cannot drive at that time of the day and night until your car has had a tune-up. The photographer (you spit the word) can take you. But I'm picking you up."

. . .

MIKA AND I talk all the way to Miami. He tells me he loves my poetry and is honored that I showed it to him. He keeps the poems in a special box at work and reads them on his break. We are soul mates. We are so in love. But no one can know this. We can't even begin to broach this truth between ourselves. We live in situations that demand our strict loyalty. Maybe this is more of my curse, my punishment, to forever live in a state of unrequited love.

As we talk, I am secretly adoring his face—his big brown eyes that remind me of Jesus (I had a big crush on Jesus when I was a child), and his prominent nose that only smart people with good breeding have, and his alabaster skin. I wish I had skin like his. I wish I could see more of it. It is so smooth, not like yours, which is old and wrinkled.

. . .

ON THE PLANE we talk about having babies. I do not know why he and Pus Head don't have any children. I don't ask. He doesn't volunteer. But we agree that in two years we can decide to have a child together. I will raise her. Mika will be very involved in her life. Child support. Moral support. Guidance.

But because he's a married man, of course he would not live with us. It would be an arrangement based on the European model.

We're just joking.

.   .   .

THIS CONVERSATION is completely stupid. We both know it. We are not going to have a child together. We are not going to act upon whatever feelings we may or may not have for one another. Mika will stay in his relationship, and I will stay in mine. That's just the way the world is.

.   .   .

TO IMAGINE THAT we will know each other two years from today, and that we will then decide whether or not to bring a child into the world is an easy, side-stepping way for us to express that we hope we are important in each other's lives.

That's all. No big deal. We are brother and sister.

.   .   .

YOU KNOW, in the eyes of the law I am single. So I have room to talk. But Mika doesn't. He is very legally married. Pus Head would be hurt if she heard us talk this way. That's it—I'm not saying anything else. I will not flirt. I will not make a fool out of myself. I will not lead Mika into temptation because anyone who can be tempted is not a good person.

. . .

Wow, we have had such a successful day! It was a good interview and Mika believes he got some great shots. We're tired, but really happy. We're having a drink on the plane. Chablis for me and scotch for Mika. Yes, scotch! That is soooo sophisticated.

I need for him to know that I'm not going to be bucktoothed forever. I reveal to him my self-improvement plan. "Every week I stash away whatever I can spare and once I have—I don't know how much it will cost—but when I've saved enough I'm going to get my teeth fixed."

Mika says, "You have beautiful teeth."

"No, no I don't."

He looks at me intently. His face is steady but a little sad. Embarrassed, I look away.

"I wish you would believe me."

"That's very nice of you. Thank you." And even though I know he's lying, I don't mind. Because it was a lie designed to make me feel good. "But it's something I really want to do."

"Then you should."

I tell him about a magazine article Heather shared with me. It was about a girl who had teeth almost as bad as mine, and she underwent maxillofacial surgery. And now she's beautiful.

"Maybe that's what I need."

"Do you have health insurance?"

"No."

He tells me that there are insurance policies designed exclusively for small businesses. He suggests I broach the topic with my publisher. I'm amazed that he knows about stuff like this. He says that, with the proper coverage, most of my surgical expenses would be paid by the insurer.

"You're kidding me? This sounds too good to be true."

"Unfortunately, insurance these days is a necessary evil."

And then we have this fascinating discussion about premiums and deductibles and the need for socialized medicine. We see eye to eye on virtually everything. He listens intently when I say, "My mother might be alive today if the system was different—if she'd had access to help."

. . .

UP HERE, twenty-five thousand feet above the earth, my shame scatters, ashlike.

. . .

YOU ARE WAITING for us as we get off the plane.

You kiss my forehead and shake Mika's hand. You are in a subdued, gentlemanly mood. You offer to buy Mika a drink. Mika accepts. He's not scared of you. This floors me.

We make our way over to the airport hotel bar. I feel sick,

as if my stomach is lined with barbed wire. No telling what you might do. I will be the peacemaker. I will keep everyone chattering and happy. Everything will be okay.

I order a glass of red wine. Mika orders scotch on the rocks. Not to be outdone, you also order a scotch. I prattle about the interview. I want you to understand that our work in Miami was strictly professional. I explain O-rings. I repeat solemnly what Mr. Rush told us: For safety equipment to be of value, the astronauts must survive the initial catastrophe.

As I jabber on you look across the room, your face impassive, a tinge of impatience deepening the long vertical lines of your face. You are bored. You think I am uninteresting. Later, you will tell me how stupid I sounded.

Nothing would make me happier than to slap you. Hard. Right across your broad cheekbones. I think I actually might do it. I think I'm losing control, that I am seconds away from beating on you. So I excuse myself and go in search of the nearest bathroom.

The Tampa airport keeps their bathrooms superclean. I can stay in here all night without worrying about catching a communicable disease. I check. All the stalls are empty. I wash my hands. I stare at my reflection. *"You have beautiful teeth."* For a little while I sort of believed Mika. I actually behaved with him as if I weren't a freak. And now that I have returned to my own private emotional wasteland, I realize that all the while he had played me for a fool.

I say to the girl in the mirror, "Don't trust anyone. Not a soul."

Then I apply a fresh coat of face powder and punch up my eye makeup. Next, some clear gloss on my lips. Then on to the hair. I rummage through my purse, looking for my brush. Mama used to have roaches in her purse. She didn't put them there. They crawled in under the cover of night. Bastards. Maybe they were after her cigarettes. I don't know. I'm dawdling too long. It isn't ladylike. I find my brush and press its bristles into the palm of my hand. Hard. It really hurts. But it's not enough to kill me. So I stop. No telling what you're saying about me. You are probably explaining to Mika what a sick, foolish child I am. I better get back out there and stop you. Try to set things straight. Make everyone happy.

.   .   .

SILLY ME. You and Mika are not discussing my stupidity or my genius. You are chatting about cameras and film speed and darkroom equipment.

The conversation is painfully civil. It's as if the two of you are in a British movie, speaking in clipped English accents, choosing every word with tweezerlike precision, the obvious dislike of the other apparent only in your leaden gazes.

So here we are, the three of us, engaged in polite blah, blah, blah conversation. Drink up, boys, before it's too late, before somebody says something we're going to regret.

But now nobody is speaking. No more camera gibberish. No more words chosen so carefully that even the air is undisturbed when they are uttered.

Tick-tock, tick-tock, tick-tock, tick-tock. This isn't good. Mean thoughts can bubble to the surface when nobody is speaking. I must make chitchat. They must finish their drinks. And then we can get out of here and everything will be A-Okay. Blurt out something, anything, whatever comes to mind.

"Heather says I ought to consult an oral surgeon. They might be able to do something about my teeth, and Mika suggested I talk to my publisher about buying health insurance. Don't you think that's a good idea?"

You suck in your lips as if they bear the residue of a delicious meal that you wish hadn't ended. Then you sip your scotch.

I think you haven't heard me so I try again. "I mean, about the insurance. We could get coverage for everybody."

You take a drag off your cigarette. You inhale deeply. Then you blow the smoke into my face. You can be very poised when you're mad, poised enough to wait for the smoke to clear, to tilt your head as if you're fascinated by my foolishness, to then explain calmly, "You are so stupid. Nobody is going to insure you. Not to get those fucking teeth fixed. The best thing anybody could do for you is to just pull them out. Jerk 'em right out of there. Face it kid, you've got buckteeth. You're ugly. Learn to live with it!"

I feel as though you have just taken a baseball bat to my brain. I can't hold back. I bawl. I can't stop. I am crushed. I am mortified. I cannot breathe.

You toss me a napkin. "Blow your fucking nose."

Next it's down the hatch with your drink. The cigarettes and bar matches disappear into a pocket. You are huge. You are no longer an old man. You are God. Very Old Testament.

"I'm going to pull the car around," you say, standing. "Meet me downstairs."

You stride away. Mika takes my hand.

"It's okay, Connie. It's okay."

I nod, unable to speak. I am such a fool. I try to regain my composure. But it is hopeless. You have destroyed me.

Mika helps me to my feet and leads me out of the hotel bar. He guides me to the elevator. He pushes the down button. The doors open. We step inside and are swiftly delivered to the valet level. A bell rings and, again, the doors open. A bellman sweeps his arm in a gesture that indicates we are to exit into the night.

"Thank you for visiting the Hyatt," he says.

Mika and I stand on the sidewalk, waiting for you to pick us up.

I am still weeping. I wish you had beaten me. I wish you had killed me. I wish you had cracked open my skull, and that I was lying dead, and that my blood was soaking into the soft gray hotel carpet. Anything other than this public humiliation. You made me into a bad person in Mika's eyes. You made me into a fool.

Where can I find instructions on how to gas myself?

That is what I'm thinking when suddenly Mika takes me in his arms, lifts me off the ground, and swings me in a full circle.

As he spins me around, he presses his lips to mine. It is so sweet, this kiss. I want to be suspended, lip to lip, in this man's arms until I am way too old for such foolish behavior.

Can a kiss be a transcendent moment? Can it whisper away our failings? Can it cast aside human pain and doubt, allowing us a glimpse at the finer details of our nature? In the span of one human sigh, can a kiss define compassion and longing and reason?

While I am in the air, in his arms, I know the answers to all of these questions. Yes. Yes. Absolutely. Yes.

But I also understand that no matter how much we might resist, my toes will touch the earth again. And when they do, I will want to rest my head against Mika's chest. I will want him to touch my hair. I will want to say, "Take me away from here. Please." But I will never get the chance. Because as soon as Mika sets me down, I see the glint of the silver Audi as you pull around the corner.

How did you get here so fast? You are an old man with stiff joints who has had much to drink. Did you run to the car? Are you so jealous of my happiness that you overcame age and alcohol in order to make quick work of my joy?

I do not know if I can make it into the car. I am reeling. I've shuttled between despair and a happy heart and back to despair with far too much speed. Mika understands this. He is a decent man. He steadies me with a discreet hand on my waist. We get in, Mika in back and me up front. I feel as if I have been split in two.

You have turned on the classical station. Before slipping

the Audi into gear, you turn up the volume loud enough to end run any possibility of conversation. For this I am grateful.

I roll down the window. The air is cool and fresh and hints of the bay which we will soon cross. I close my eyes. I want my other life back, the one that flourished during the mere width of a kiss. In the air I was free. In the air I was not a freak. I press myself against the seat. In the dark, Mika slips his hand onto my shoulder. I sneak my hand into his. He does not let go.

This is life lived dangerously. This is a life where one says yes to possibilities.

This is a life that could kill me.

.   .   .

ALONE, in the privacy of my office, I open my desk drawer and pull out my covert, neatly typed "What I Am" list.

Editor. Writer. Journalist. Cook . . .

I add *pathetic*.

Then I cross it out. Then I decide the entire list is stupid. Disgusted, I draw a giant *X* across the page.

I grab a fresh sheet of paper and a blue magic marker. I write "Who I Want To Be."

But then I don't write anything else. I just sit. And stare.

I could lie. I could write *Movie Star*. Or *Newspaper Columnist*. Or *Patti Smith*. Or *Radio Engineer*.

Why can't the truth be simple? Inane? Like when Bob Barker interviews Miss America contestants. I mean, he could ask something outrageous such as, "Would you like to get down on all fours naked and bark like a dog?" and each and every beauty queen would answer, smiling brilliantly with the aid of Vaseline-smeared teeth, "Yes."

Everyone would clap.

Everyone would love them.

But at this moment, in my little hovel of an office, with no one else around, if Bob Barker asked me, "Who do you want to be?" I'd have to tell the truth.

And then it would be out in the open, and no one would clap. Jaws would drop. Some people would boo.

Because my truth is a negative, sort of like an X ray of my intent.

The truth makes me ashamed. The truth could be a big sin. The truth is unspeakable.

But at least I finally recognize it.

I write in big blue letters I DON'T WANT TO BE MY MAMA.

. . .

YOU ARE IN BED, asleep. Your mouth is open and you are snoring. I could stuff your mouth full of socks. Or razor blades. How surprised you would be!

But I won't do that. Of course not. That would be insane.

Instead, in this room that seems to change shape in tandem with the flickering light of the TV, I study you and wonder. You are so much older than me. May-September romances only work if the man is rich. Like Bing Crosby.

Plus, his wife has those silly movies he made with Bob Hope to remind her of when he was young and handsome.

Was your skin ever smooth? Your face unlined? Were you virile? Did you make girls swoon? When you were my age, did you dream of having a wife and children? Did you see the world as a place full of possibilities? Could you not even glimpse death, it being so many years away?

I walk over to the closet and rummage through it until I find the box, the one filled with a hodgepodge of dog-eared photographs. I have looked at them before. In fact, I do so often. I don't know why I'm drawn to them. I suppose it's because I view them as clues. Yes, these faded images of you are trying to tell me something.

They are all so familiar. You on stage in a play. You with your wife and newborn baby. You with your family on vacation. You interviewing Mel Tormé in a jazz station in Miami Beach.

I study the images closely. No doubt about it, you certainly were a handsome man. I look over my shoulder at the real you, an old drunk in a stupored sleep. I shove the box back into the closet. I will not shuffle through its contents again. There is no need. Because now I know what the photographs have been trying to tell me: You have lived your life.

.　.　.

I AM going to try to live mine.

.　.　.

I MAKE THE PHONE CALL from my office when no one is
around. My hands are shaking, that's how nervous I am. And
when I speak, the words feel heavy in my mouth, as if they're
too bloated with hope and fear to roll off my tongue with any
grace.

"I'm interested in getting braces."

"Do you mind if I ask how old you are?"

"I'm in my twenties."

"Well, you'll be glad to know that we have many adult
patients."

.　.　.

THE ORTHODONTIST says the doctor I visited when I was
fourteen was telling the truth when he said he couldn't
help me.

"We were in the dark ages back then, orthodontically
speaking. Today, there's barely anything we can't fix." He
smiles. His teeth are white and straight and I'm sure he
flosses daily.

I'm not a good conversationalist. So I just nod and try to
appear fascinated when what I am, truly, is scared speech-
less. This is only the second time in my life that I have been
to a dentist or an orthodontist. No telling what all is wrong in
there.

He claps his hands together once, and says, "Okay, let's take a look."

There are many forms of rape. Of intimate bodily violation coupled with mental anguish. Yes, I know the doctor is doing his job. He is very professional. He's not trying to hurt me. But I have spent my entire life hiding my deformity. And he is doing everything he can to poke, prod, and expose it. Photographs are taken. Measurements are made. Teeth are tapped. I bite into a mass of gummy clay that tastes slightly of gasoline. I want to gag. But he needs that impression. He's sorry. He knows it's uncomfortable. ". . . but it can't be helped. It will be over soon. You'll hear a popping sound when I take it out. That's it. Good. You're doing very, very well."

By the time he is done, my lips feel so profoundly pulled out of shape I'm certain I resemble Wiley Coyote with a mouth full of dynamite.

The doctor gives me a fatherly pat on the shoulder, and then tells the nurse to finish up. He leaves us alone, and the nurse instructs me to swish and spit. It's demeaning, swishing and spitting in public. But I guess people do it all the time.

When I'm done, she escorts me back to the doctor's office which is filled with goofy teeth paraphernalia. A big plastic molar pencil holder. A jaw paperweight. A set of false teeth hinged on a spring that holds telephone messages in its bite. A needlepoint wall plaque: BRUSH TWICE A DAY EVERY DAY! There's also a snapshot of him with his perfect family. A skinny wife with a big hairdo and two perfect children. A boy and a girl, of course.

He tells me to sit down. I feel as though I've been summoned to the principal's office. I'm trying to appear pleasant, unafraid, and as if my pockets are loaded with cash.

As he looks at his notes, he says, "This is definitely doable, but braces alone aren't the answer." He looks up but avoids meeting my eye. It's not good to look patients in the eye. Too intimate. "In fact, your teeth are in pretty good shape. It's your jaw that's the problem. It's severely malformed. For the braces to do their job, we have to bring the upper and lower jaws into alignment. This can only be done through surgery."

I thought I was prepared for this. I mean, Heather showed me the magazine article with the before and after shots of that lady who resembled a monkey until her surgery transformed her into a babe. But, still, to hear my problem explained in such no-nonsense terms steals from me the balm of ignorance. I can't run from it. I can't sugarcoat it. This is it, this is the answer. I so wish it were simpler. I wish all I had to do was push on my teeth like my mama said. And I so wish he hadn't described my jaw as malformed.

But I don't act like I'm upset or anything. I listen very carefully, even though my brain is filled with a far-off screaming noise. I hear him and understand that I have to go to a maxillofacial surgeon, and that he and the surgeon will come up with a game plan after they have a better idea of the extent of my jaw irregularity. Between surgery and braces, the entire process will take anywhere from two to five years. We just don't know yet. *We just don't know yet. We just don't know yet.*

I get in my car and head back to my office, and I don't tell anyone where I've been. I try to work on my profit and loss statement, but all I can think is, *I am deformed. I am a freak. It's not my fault. I was born this way.*

.   .   .

WHEN I GET HOME, supper is on the table. You have bought Chinese food from the place down on Fourth Street. You are wearing new clothes. Blue linen pants and a beige sports shirt. New slip-on shoes, too. You fill your water glass with wine and ask me about my day. You are acting real nice, like you care about me. You must want something.

I feed Katie a noodle and say, "I went to an orthodontist today. He wants me to see a surgeon." I toss this out there like it doesn't matter.

You do not appear to be surprised that I have taken my deformity into my own hands. Instead, belying your mean- ness of a few nights ago, you say, "I've got the guy for you. I did a few shows with him. Best surgeon in town, kiddo."

.   .   .

I DON'T UNDERSTAND why you are being nice about the surgery thing. Maybe you were wanting me to make the decision on my own. Maybe your humiliation of me was an attempt to make me stick up for myself. Maybe it was tough love.

You take me to the surgeon and stay with me through all of the exam except for the X-ray part. You ask questions and behave very concerned and I am touched.

At the end of the appointment, the surgeon renders his verdict. My lower jaw has never sat properly in the joint, and it is wearing away. It is not my imagination that over the years my overbite seems to be getting worse. It is getting worse. My bone is disintegrating.

"If you are not in pain now," the surgeon assures me, "you soon will be."

His plan is to put me in braces which will realign my teeth and, once that is done, I will undergo surgery in which he will break my lower jaw, swing it forward, and secure it with steel plates. He might also have to throw in a prosthetic or two—something about stabilizing or filling out my chin. I will be wired shut for approximately one month. I will have a splint in my mouth. I will only be able to eat through a straw. You can eat anything through a straw if you liquify it. He had one patient who put an entire Thanksgiving dinner in a blender and afterward claimed it was mighty tasty. Post-surgery, I will not automatically be beautiful. There will be swelling and bruising. And, oh yes, I will remain in braces for an unknown period of time. Anywhere from one to three years.

I decide, *Fuck it. I'm not doing this. I don't want someone to break my jaw and screw in steel plates. I don't want to suck turkey through a straw. Are they crazy? I'm not going to let this guy carve me up. What if his hands aren't all that steady? What if he maims me? What if I die on the operating table with my face cut open? None of my suicide plans ever involved disfiguration.*

I'm going to learn to be happy just the way I am. "I'm really not convinced this is necessary."

To prove me wrong, the surgeon whips out his photo album and starts the hard sell. He tells me each person's heart-wrenching story. I can't take my eyes off the images. The photos say it all. This surgeon is a master. A true artist. Better than God. He transforms freaks into perfect human beings. Some of them look so gorgeous postsurgery they could be movie stars. None of them, I'm positive, ever get called names anymore. I look at photo after photo and despite my best efforts at remaining icy calm, the tears start.

I want to be perfect, too. I want to be made whole. No matter what it costs or how long it takes or how much it hurts, I will do this. I will let this man turn me into someone who looks like everyone else.

.   .   .

YOU WERE RIGHT. No one is jumping at the opportunity to insure me.

I don't mention why I want the insurance. I simply behave like the head of a small business who is trying to do right by her employees.

But I don't fool them. They take one look at me and say, "We'll have to put an exclusion on your policy."

They don't detail what type of exclusion. We both know what they mean.

I tell Heather and George my troubles. They have become good friends. They don't even seem to mind that you don't like them. Heather explains it very calmly, "He sees us as a threat. You're blossoming and he doesn't know how to handle it so he blames us."

That's what is amazing about Heather and George. They always seem to have the answers to my problems. No photographer? Here's Mika. No decent insurance? Meet our friend, Fred.

Fred, it turns out, is a Buddhist who sells insurance on the side. He has long hair and wears Birkenstocks. He has decided, he tells me, to mess with the system from within.

I tell him about the plans for my face (he's not someone you can lie to) and he says, "We just won't write that part down."

. . .

In three days I will drive myself over to the orthodontist's office, and I will sit in the exam chair for several hours while I am fitted with braces. I have dreamed of this moment since I was a little girl. I won't be ashamed to walk around with a mouth full of metal, because having braces is like saying to the world, "See, here, I'm improving myself."

The orthodontist wants a two-hundred-and-fifty-dollar deposit. Then I pay monthly. Fifty bucks. This is no problem. I've been stashing money in my secret account. I've been very disciplined. I think that by now I should have about eight thousand dollars saved. That's enough to pay for my braces and is a start for whatever the insurance won't cover when I have my surgery.

But have I really saved that much money? I should be better about keeping track. I should know how much I have, down to the very last dime. Maybe I've saved more than I realize. Maybe I could buy some new clothes.

. . .

I KEEP THE bank statements hidden in an old tin can on the top shelf of the kitchen behind three bags of flour. I pull over a wooden chair, climb on it, and on my tiptoes reach for the tin.

If you come home, the dogs will bark before you've even reached the front door. You will not discover my deceit. The dogs will buy me time.

. . .

STANDING AT MY kitchen counter, I rifle through the statements, looking for the most recent one. When I find it, I slit open the envelope with a paring knife. I remove the state ment and press the paper flat against the cabinet door. I search for a little box that says Ending Balance. There it is, in solid black ink. Twenty-five hundred dollars. That doesn't make sense.

I rip open the other statements. I put them in order. I start at the beginning. Everything looks fine. For twelve months, the account steadily grows. But two months ago money starts being withdrawn. Three thousand dollars in one week alone.

You could not know about this account. There is no way. The statements come to my office. This is the bank's mistake. I look up at my wall clock. It's six-fifteen. The bank is closed. I will go first thing in the morning. I will not behave hysterically. I will explain calmly that there has been a bookkeeping error. I have my deposit slips to prove it.

Everything will be okay. Everything will be okay. Everything will be okay.

Dear God, don't let him come home tonight. Maybe, God, you can do me a favor and strike him dead.

I could leave now with my twenty-five hundred dollars. But then I'd have to explain to my publisher about you. And she rented this house to me. Your name is not on the lease. Yes, I would have to tell her all about you and that is not possible. Telling the truth would be the deepest form of betrayal. After all, I'm not a very good person. Just like Mama said. Just like you always say. Nobody else can love me. Why would I betray the only person capable of putting up with me? Besides, if I used the money to move, what would I do about my braces? Or my surgery?

I'm too close to blow it now. *Just stay cool. Everything will be okay.*

.   .   .

I AM SITTING ON the porch watching the fireflies, plotting how to force you to confess.

Katie jumps on my lap and licks my face. She buries her head in my chest and we snuggle. I hug her hard. She doesn't seem to mind. I scold myself. Of course you didn't steal my money. What a rotten thing for me to think.

.   .   .

KATIE AND I lie on the couch. She sleeps curled up against my belly. I watch the light change as it filters in through the front windows. When there is more light than shadow, Katie stirs. I get up and take a shower.

You have not returned, and I'm too spent to care. I get dressed and feed the dogs and drink some coffee and wish that I could call Mika and ask him what he thinks about my missing money. But I can't call him. He is a married man even if the marriage is in tatters. Besides, why should I trust him? Why should I trust anybody?

It is six-thirty in the morning. The bank isn't open yet. I

need to kill time. I need to try to steady my nerves. So I go out to my porch room and sit at the desk and begin to organize my interview tapes. This is an easy task. Just a matter of alphabetizing. *A, B, C, D.* Nothing to it. By 8:00 A.M. I'm waiting in the bank parking lot.

.   .   .

I HAVE ALL MY statements with me. I lay them out on the bank officer's desk. My hands are shaking.

This is a woman in her forties. She wears lots of rings (mostly sapphires), that must be her birthstone. She makes me nervous. Older women usually do.

"I like your rings."

She looks up from her computer screen and a smile briefly cracks her businesslike demeanor. "Oh! Thank you," she says and then she returns her attention to the monitor. She makes clucking noises. She is real good on the keyboard. Her fingers, which are crowned with fake pink nails, fly. I wonder if she can play piano.

Her printer kicks in. She turns to me. "I'm printing out the withdrawal records."

I don't say a word. I am tongue-tied. I'm grateful when the printer falls silent and she shoves the thin paper in front of me.

She uses her flawlessly manicured index finger as a pointer as she explains the activity in my account month by month.

"Oh, I see. I see. I must have forgotten." I try to keep my face steady, but I'm afraid my bottom lip is quivering.

She must be thinking, *Only an idiot doesn't remember withdrawing six grand.*

"Thank you. I'm so sorry to have taken up your time."

"Not at all. That's why I'm here."

I gather up the bank statements and head to the door, thinking I might vomit or that my legs will go out from under me and I'll just lie in the lobby, sobbing, and they'll call an ambulance that will take me to a mental ward, and a handsome single psychiatrist will fall in love with me.

Oh dear Jesus, you have stolen nearly six thousand dollars from me in just over two months. If it weren't my surgery money, maybe this wouldn't hurt so bad.

·   ·   ·

I GO TO WORK and behave as though I'm a human dynamo. I make phone calls. I assign stories. I write my column. I decide our printing bill is too high, so I call two other printers and request bids. I clean off my desk. I organize my pencils, paper clips, glue sticks, what-have-you into tiny worlds of their own. I flip through my Rolodex and decide it needs to be updated. I pore over old notes and phone messages, culling names and numbers and filling out Rolodex cards with careful cursive script. I double-check to make sure all entries, old and new, are alphabetized correctly. I skip lunch.

Your name does not cross my lips. When your face mate-
rializes in my mind's eye, I squash it.

.   .   .

I LEAVE WORK and head straight for home. I need to feed and
walk the dogs. I need to hold on to Katie. I decide that if
you're home I simply won't speak to you.

But what am I worried about? Of course you're not home.
You're out spending my surgery money.

.   .   .

KATIE AND I walk down to the bay. We sit on the bench and
stare at the water. She barks at birds.

When we get home, God smells her butt, her mouth, her
haunches.

"Now you know everything," I tell him.

.   .   .

I DO NOT WANT to be alone tonight. I'm afraid that I'll start
watching the clock and running to the window to see if the
car coming down the street is your silver Audi. And that if I
do, that I won't be able to bear myself.

So I get in my car and head over to Heather and George's.

Because the stolen money is yet another point of shame,

I do not tell them about it. All I say is, "Y'all want to catch some dinner?" And they say "Sure." Your name never comes up.

.   .   .

You are home when I return. I do not ask you where you have been. You do not volunteer the information. But you do demand to know what the hell I've been up to.

"I had dinner with Heather and George."

You look at me as if exasperated by my naivete.

"You are such a slut."

"How does having dinner with two friends make me a slut?"

"Because they're using you!"

"*They're* using me!"

You take a deep breath and ball your fists.

I realize I've just stepped onto very thin ice. I move out of striking range. I sit on the couch, and Katie jumps up and lies down with her head in my lap. I rub her ears.

You go into the kitchen and come back with a bottle of wine. You pour yourself a drink. You say that big things are happening with the screenplay. You say you will probably have to go to L.A.

I don't say a word. I just hang on to Katie. She is steady and good, two things I need to be right now.

"Aren't you happy? I'm doing this for us."

I nod yes. "I'm happy. I'm just a little tired is all."

"Well, kiddo, that's what you get for living the life!"

You light a cigarette and pour more wine. You're drinking fast. You put your feet up on the table. You hold your cigarette between gritted teeth as if you've got the whole world figured out. You glance over at me, seemingly amused. Maybe you find my stupidity, my gullibility, vastly entertaining.

I want to shout, "What did you do with my money?" But I can't. Confrontation is not in the cards. I bury my face in Katie's thick black coat.

You take your cigarette out of your mouth and shout excitedly, "I've got it! Listen to this, kid. I had lunch today with our M.S. pal."

"Oh?"

"He's got a new girlfriend."

"That's good."

"No! That's not the good part. This is: The M.S. has made him impotent. Five whores working at one time couldn't help him get it up. So he goes to the doc, see, and the doc gives him this medication that he's supposed to inject into his cock to make himself hard. Is that great or what!"

You are giggling hysterically. I'm horrified.

"He puts a needle in his penis?"

"Yeah, but that's not even the half of it!" You are really rolling now. You seem giddy. You pour the last of the wine and take a giant gulp. I'm still stuck on how anyone could give themselves a shot in that place when you say, "He's going to give me some!"

"Some of what?"

"The hard-on medicine! I know what you need. You're a young woman. I'm going to give it to you. You won't be hanging out with your so-called friends once I get my hands on you."

Why are you giggling? Why is any of this funny to you? You can't be serious about this medicine thing. You're just joking around. The wine has put you in a silly mood. That's all. But I don't feel safe right now. I need to get away.

I stand and you say, "Darling, get me another bottle, please."

Katie follows me into the kitchen. I kneel down and pet her. "We're going to be okay," I whisper, but this time I don't believe in the words at all.

.   .   .

You will not fuck me. I will kill myself first.

I open the medicine cabinet. I move aside Band-Aids, Visine, cough syrup. I find the razor blades beneath a box of Sudafed.

If I do this, it will be final, decisive. I don't want people to say, "Look at all those hesitation marks. She didn't really want to die."

I will make a single, deep slash. At each wrist. Symmetry, you see. What I do to one side I must do to the other.

I bring the razor to the pale vein-etched skin of my left wrist.

Mama believed suicide was a sin. This never made sense to me. I asked her, "Why is it a sin, Mama?"

"Because God doesn't want you to kill yourself," she explained. "If you do, He sends you straight to Hell."

If God sends suicides to Hell, where does He send murderers? Or rapists? Or child molesters? I thought God was supposed to take care of the wounded and sad.

This sucks. It all absolutely sucks.

Katie huffs and lies on her side. She's sleepy.

"Hey, sweet Katie."

She wags her tail twice. *Thump. Thump.*

What am I doing? I don't want to kill myself. Not really. Not in my heart.

I'm not the loser in this situation. Say it! I am not the loser.

.   .   .

IN MY CUBBYHOLE office, Mika and I drink coffee and discuss the next cover feature. It will be an interview with Frank Borman, the former astronaut who flew around the dark side of the moon and who is now CEO of Eastern Airlines.

"I asked his press agent if Borman would be coming to our side of the state any time soon. He isn't, so it looks like we'll have to travel to Miami again."

"That's great. Let's do it! When are we going?"

I flip open my calendar. I'm trying to push away the

following facts: Number one, I get goo-goo-eyed every time Mika is near. And number two, I can't wait to get on another plane with him. Maybe I should buy one-way tickets.

"We'll have to go before the end of the month. How about two weeks from Friday?"

"Yeah. Just let me check at work, but I think that will be fine." Then he taps his index finger on the calendar and says, "What's this? You're getting your braces on tomorrow? Why didn't you tell me?"

"It's no big deal."

"Yes it is, Connie. It's a really big deal."

I glance up at him and then look away. I don't want to like Mika. I don't want to trust him. I don't want to get burned. I don't want to make another mistake. I especially don't want to get involved with a married man. Come back and talk to me when you're single. There's no room in my bloody life for him. Why doesn't he just go home and patch things up with his wife?

These are my thoughts. And they are so sudden, so stubborn, so full-bodied, that I'm about to say I'm really busy and need to get back to work. I'll brush him off. Give him a very professional cold shoulder. But before the words are formed, a clap of thunder shakes my office's thin walls. I hear the rain. It's coming down hard.

"Did you drive the beater?"

"Sure did." He reaches over for the coffeepot and pours us some more.

I can't help myself. A grin slips across my face. See, that

old Volvo of his doesn't have wipers. So no matter what I try to convince myself I want, he isn't going anywhere.

. . .

There is nothing glamorous about having braces put on. That's what I'm thinking as the orthodontist says, "Just a little while longer."

I've been sitting here all morning. My stomach is growling. My jaw is aching. My teeth are throbbing. I can't open any wider. I think my lips might split. Other than that, I'm just fine. Maybe this is easier when you're twelve. Kids are more resilient than adults.

Another patient comes in and sits in the exam chair next to mine. I can't see her because the doctor is fitting a Buick into my mouth.

I know she's there, though, because the doctor says, "Hello, Mrs. Harris. I'll be with you in just a moment." And then to me, "Mrs. Harris is our oldest patient."

He pauses to find some other torture device. I look over at Mrs. Harris. My God, she *is* older than mud. I can't believe it. She smiles at me. Her mouth is full of steel.

"Hi, there," she says. "Don't you worry at all. It hurts at first, but you'll get used to it. Besides, you're young."

Mrs. Harris is not. She's the picture-perfect grandma. White hair, kind blue eyes, a floral print dress with a lace collar, and sensible black shoes. She must be eighty if she's a day. I can't help myself. I have to ask.

"Why do you have braces?" The part I leave out is, *At your age you ought to be in dentures.*

"I always wanted perfect teeth. But I couldn't afford them until now." She speaks with a soft, southern lilt. It's an accent that conjures up images of lemonade and sugar cookies, verandas and magnolias. "I don't regret it one bit, either. Every day when I wake up, I look in the mirror, and I ask it, "Mirror, mirror on the wall, who's the prettiest girl in the nursing home?"

"Does it answer you back?"

"No. Not yet. But it will. Once I'm done with these things." She flashes her full-metal grin again and taps her front tooth.

I settle back into the chair, not quite knowing what to make of Mrs. Harris, when my doctor, brandishing what looks to be a Vice-Grip, orders, "Open wide."

.   .   .

MY MOUTH IS SWOLLEN. My teeth are so tender I cannot eat solid food. I'm sitting in front of the TV with a bottle of aspirin and a tumbler full of ice and white wine. I hold the cold wine in my mouth until it becomes warm and then I swallow. The relief is temporary.

Katie is walking around the living room, stalking a fly. I'm watching "Entertainment Tonight." I hate Mary Hart. I hate John Tesch. Maybe all that hair spray has calcified their brains. Or maybe they are actually androids and the two of them have android sex by inserting their microphones in each other's portals. "Back to you, John! Thank you, Mary!"

You want to be on "Entertainment Tonight." You think you are going to write a screenplay that will make you rich and famous. You say you will share the fame and money with me. Well, I'm figuring out that I don't want your fame or your money—neither of which you will probably ever have. In my present tooth-tender mood, I'm thinking that all I want from you is the money you've stolen.

Right as I have this thought, the dogs start barking and I hear you coming up the porch steps. You stumble through the front door, a jug of wine in hand, and I see that you're three sheets to the wind.

You stagger over to me, cooing, "Oh darling!" You try to kiss me, but I push you away.

"It hurts," I explain.

"You wanted 'em, you got 'em." You lean forward and with nicotine-stained fingers pull my upper lip away from my teeth. You start laughing. "Jesus, that's a bunch of metal, kiddo."

Fuck you.

You flop down on the couch and say, "Weeeee! I've had a great day!"

Katie has given up on the fly. She and God are milling about the room. I call her over. She lies down by my feet. God brings you his tennis ball, and you toss it across the room. He slides on the wood floor and the area rugs scatter.

You reach for a dirty glass that has sat on the coffee table for I don't know how long (a few days) and you open your jug and pour.

"What's up?" I ask.

"Big stuff, darling. I mean really big."

You lean forward and rest your elbows on your knees. You wipe your mouth and look over my head as though you are gazing into the heavens.

"I'm going to L.A. The producer wants me out there. We're going to work together. Finish the screenplay. Decide on actors. Schedules. That sort of thing."

"Really?"

"Yeah! Isn't it great! We're going to make it, baby!"

I want to believe you. I want to believe with every cell of my body that you are not a liar.

"When do you go?"

"Tomorrow."

"Really? That soon."

"This is big stuff."

"Do you have tickets?"

You pull your cigarettes from your breast pocket and fiddle with them before lighting one. You take a long drag, flick the ash on the floor, and say, "I need to borrow a couple of thousand dollars for the trip. I thought we could stop by the bank on the way to the airport."

"Why don't you just take it, like you did the other money?" In my mind, I'm daring you to hit me.

You look hurt. Or maybe you're surprised that I've gathered enough nerve to confront you.

"I spent that money for us! Do you think convincing these assholes to make my movie is cheap?"

"The money is for my surgery."

"Oh fuck you, lady."

You stand and start to pace.

"Why can't you get it through your thick skull that once this film is made we'll be able to fix not only your mouth, but anything else you want done! Your ass. Your tits. Anything!"

And then you start. But your repertoire of accusations has grown stale. I've heard them so many times. First from my mother and now from you. I am stupid. I am ungrateful. You have sacrificed everything for me. You are doing all of this for me. All I do is use you, use you, use you.

Suddenly you grab me by my T-shirt and pull me to my feet. Katie starts barking.

"Listen to me, you cunt, can't you just do this one goddamn thing for me!"

You shove me, and I fall back into the chair. Katie jumps in my lap and accidently bangs her head into my mouth.

"Ow!"

"What! What!" You slap me. "What's wrong with you!"

I am in excruciating pain. The braces have created

tiny cuts on the inside of my mouth and your blow has split them open.

"Well?"

I start to cry. My toughness dissolves. The accusations are all true. I am unworthy. I didn't mean to upset you. I wish I could be a better person.

"You can have anything I have. You know that. I am so sorry."

"Aw, it's okay, kid." You rub your hand across my cheek, but Katie bares her teeth and snaps.

You laugh and sit back down. Before nursing your drink you say, "That's a hell of a dog you've got there."

.   .   .

THE NEXT MORNING, on the way to the airport, we stop at the bank. You repeat that figure, *two thousand dollars*. "But that leaves me with only five hundred and that is my surgery mo—"

"For Christ's sake, shut up! I know it's your surgery money. And I've told you until I'm sick of it that you're going to have all the money you could ever want. Just help me out here!"

I withdraw the money and hand it to you without comment. You tuck it into the inside breast pocket of your sports coat. "Thanks, kiddo."

The morning traffic is heavy. I try to concentrate on driving rather than on the fact that you are, once more, rendering me broke.

My mouth is throbbing. I need to take more Tylenol. I run my tongue across my braces. They feel knobby and cold. I hope the cuts on the inside of my mouth don't get infected. I'm supposed to rinse three times daily with salt water. I won't do it. I hate salt water.

I glance over at you. You are studying your nails. They're so shiny with that clear polish. Imagine that, a grown man getting a manicure. You look girly.

"Nice polish."

"Thank you, my dear."

"You're welcome."

Jerk. I hope you never come back.

.   .   .

I'M AT THE OFFICE, drinking a Diet Coke and holding a cold compress to my mouth to try to ease the swelling, when Mika walks in with the proofs for the upcoming cover.

He's wearing a black T-shirt and faded blue jeans. His hair is messed up from the wind. I think his looks are to die for. He congratulates me on getting the braces. He says they look nice on me. He asks if they are painful.

I start to answer but the words won't come. Suddenly I feel completely overwhelmed, as if I'm lost in a blizzard of conflicts and dicey moral dilemmas. Bad choices and fate have landed me here. Barely two feet away stands the object of my desire, but I cannot even enjoy his company. The possibilities hurt too much.

.   .   .

You have been gone for five days.

I do not miss you.

Maybe you'll have a heart attack and die.

.   .   .

I have thrown out all of your booze bottles, just like I did the night Mama died. I have mopped the floors, scrubbed the woodwork, washed the windows.

Your scent must be neutralized. Also, your ashes. Your nicotine haze that stains clothing and wallboard and crystal. The sound of you hacking up phlegm each morning. All these reminders must be erased. My disgusting whimper "please don't hit me," needs to be silenced.

You are too much like my mother. I know this now.

.   .   .

Katie and I take long walks. The December air is fresh and cold. Sometimes we jog along the bay front. After work I take her for rides in my Triumph. I keep a good grip on her lead. She is a spontaneous little girl. I don't want her leaping out of the car after a cat or a man in uniform. She hates men in uniforms. Cops. UPS. Mail carriers. I think she has an authority complex.

.   .   .

I HAVE FINALLY lost my mind. With you a continent away, it is easy for me to behave as if you do not exist.

This mind trick allows me astonishing freedoms.

Sometimes I take Katie with me to the office at night, and she sleeps at my feet while I catch up on my work.

Last night I ate a pickle sandwich for supper. It was delicious.

Without a second thought, I routinely pop in on Heather and George. I stay as long as I want.

I sleep well.

I'm not afraid all of the time.

Everything has a downside, however. The insanity your absence has induced causes me to behave recklessly. And I cannot afford reckless behavior. Not when it is with Mika.

But I cannot stop myself. He has an ease about him that I slip into without the slightest hesitation. I lecture myself about his marital status and our professional relationship and the toll that indiscretions demand of the soul, but I can't lock him out. God knows, I keep trying. If I were to grade myself I would get an A for effort and an F for execution.

I am wildly happy that he is driving the two of us to Sarasota on work-related business. Giddy, in fact, even though my brain tells me that this is a man who could severely rattle my world if I do not rein in my careless heart.

But here we are, he and I, in a city where no one knows us. We can be anyone here. We can be best friends. We can be lovers. We can pretend that we are free. The light in Sarasota is very intense. It bleaches away shadows. Here everything gleams.

So, I conduct the interview. Mika photographs the subject. We do a good job. We work well together, he and I. And then Mika takes me to lunch. At St. Armand's Key, a chi-chi shopping area in Sarasota that rises in jeweled tones of terracotta and cobalt at the ruffled edge of the Gulf.

We share a bottle of wine. We nibble on trendy food. People think we are a couple. I am grossly happy.

We do not talk about my home life or his. We pretend I am not a battered woman living with a monstrous human who is thirty years older than me and who steals from me my joy and money and good sense. We pretend he isn't trapped in a dead marriage. We pretend he has never told me about living with a woman who is, he says, cold and disapproving and judgmental. We pretend that he and I have a future. Worse than that, we pretend as if we have a life.

"Your poetry is wonderful," he says. "It moves me to tears."

"Oh, no, really, I'm not a very good poet. I'm just a scribbler." I look down at my lap. I don't know how to accept compliments. I think they are lies.

He reaches across the table and gently strokes my cheek.

"You are a beautiful woman," he says. "I wish I could convince you."

My brain shuts down, barring any possibility of a response. But my heart, that unruly child, does not miss a beat: *You can. You can. You can.*

. . .

IT IS NEARLY ten o'clock by the time we get back to St. Petersburg. We head over to Heather and George's because that is where I have left my car. There are no lights on in their apartment.

"They must be asleep," I say.

"Must be."

We watch in silence as the traffic light on the corner flashes from red to green. I know I should say something witty, sophisticated, intelligent, thought-provoking. And then I should hurry out of this car. But I'm stumped.

I start to mumble, "Thank you. I had a really nice time," but the words remain only an impulse because Mika reaches over, takes my face in his hands, and kisses me.

It is not the first kiss between him and me, but it is a significant kiss nevertheless. It is during this kiss that we stop trying to please anyone but ourselves.

We are hungry. Finally, we are doing what we've wanted since the moment we laid eyes on each other. He flips the seat lever and back we go. I am unbuttoning his shirt. He pulls my blouse over my head. I release the waist button on his jeans. He shimmies out of them as if shedding a useless skin. He is hard, he has no flab. Not like me. I'm a softy—all curves and moon-white skin. He is beautiful. His narrow hips fit perfectly in the curved bowl of my pelvis. The wind rustles through our hair.

. . .

How could we? How could Mika do such a thing to his wife, even if the marriage is on the rocks? How could I have crossed that sacred line? How in the world could I have cheated on you?

And what's worse is that I loved every second of last night. I replay it over and over in my head, savoring the sweet details.

Sure, I'm scared about what we did. Scared that I got something I wanted. Scared about where it may or may not lead. Guilty of a moral crime, perhaps even ashamed. But goddamn me all to hell because I cannot summon one ounce of regret for having done it.

. . .

God paces at the foot of the bed. He wants to be fed. I rub Katie's belly. She rests her head on my shoulder and gazes at me adoringly.

"Mama did a bad thing last night," I whisper.

She gives my cheek a slobbery lick. I hold her muzzle and shower it with little kisses as if she were a baby. God jumps on the bed, and Katie immediately moves away.

I get out of bed and let them out to pee. I fix their dog bowls and then put on a pot of coffee. I flip open the phone book and look up your son's phone number. He likes the pup. He said if he were his, he'd rename him Bud.

"Hi. It's Connie . . . No I haven't heard from your dad but I'm sure he's fine. You know, he always is . . . Listen, do you still want the dog?"

.   .   .

I'M IN MY PAJAMAS, sitting in the kitchen, drinking coffee, reading the paper, trying not to think about Mika or the mess I've gotten into with him, when there is a knock at the front door.

The dogs go crazy. I hate uninvited visitors. If I sit here long enough, maybe they will go away.

They knock again. This time louder. Shit, maybe it's Mika! Maybe he left The Wife and has come over to tell me.

I am so fucking gullible. Of course, he hasn't left his wife. People don't just walk out. Do they?

No. These things take time.

I get up and peak through the window. A florist's van is parked in front of the house. I zip out of the kitchen, push past the dogs, and fling open the door.

"Ms. May?"

"Yes." I step outside, shutting the door behind me. The dogs continue to bark.

"Flowers for you." He holds out the vase.

"Really?" No one has ever sent me flowers before. I don't know what to do. "Are you sure they're for me?"

"Are you Connie May?"

"Yes."

"Well, then, they're yours. Here," he says as if speaking to a moron.

I take the vase from him. It is overflowing with an exuberant mix of daylilies and other flowers I cannot name.

"Who sent them?"

"There's a card in it. See, right here."

"Wow. Well, okay. Thanks."

I wave good-bye so he knows he can go and then shove my way back into the house. The dogs jump on me.

"Off! Off!"

I set the vase on the coffee table and slip the card out of its tiny envelope. *To my beautiful Connie.* The card is signed simply, *Me.* It is Mika's handwriting—I know that penmanship, that slanted to the right and tightly angular scrawl. I press the card to my heart and leap around the room.

He did not use me. I did not use him. We were figuring things out. We were simply saying yes to the journey. Hold on to that thought.

·   ·   ·

AT RANDOM MOMENTS throughout this day, when my guilt and shame and worry ebb, I will gaze at the flowers and take in their scent and trace the curves of each petal, and I will think about Mika, about how beautifully he moved in the moonlight.

.   .   .

IT IS JUST Katie and me now. The pup is gone, having been adopted by your son.

Katie seems ecstatic. She brings me her toys. She plays fetch and catch. She lies on her back and wiggles to and fro. She leaps to her feet and smiles.

I think she was tired of being bullied.

.   .   .

IT'S OFFICIAL. Mika and I are having an affair. We have trysts in secret places. We lunch in dark, out-of-the-way cafés. We agonize over the unknowable future.

In my positive moments, I think that we are simply try-ing to understand life. You know, how to take control of it, how to determine our destiny for ourselves rather than let-ting the past or others determine it for us. And though I want to play by the rules, I have discovered that sometimes life doesn't allow it.

Here's the flip side. In my negative moments, I am ashamed. I call myself names. Fool. Hussy. Bad—I'm a very bad person. And I fear that Mika will actually turn out not to be all of the things he appears to be: earnest, thoughtful, sensitive, caring, talented, funny. And if that's true, when all is said and done, the only thing I will have earned from our time together is bitterness.

I am a moral person. But does morality allow any wiggle room? Can two people be held accountable for their sin if they commit that sin with good and fair hearts?

. . .

MIKA SAYS they sleep in separate bedrooms. And that they live separate lives. And that he is consulting an attorney about divorce proceedings.

I do not know if any of this is true. It is not my place to know. I cannot make demands or issue ultimatums. I'm in no position.

Besides, I understand perhaps more than most how difficult leaving someone is.

In fact, when I leave you, it won't be because I've found another man. It's going to be because I finally value myself enough that I won't allow your poison into my life.

In short, what I am beginning to understand is this: I have to learn how to take responsibility for my own happiness, for my own sense of self-worth, for my own idea of what my place in the world should be.

Mika and Heather and George might help me figure these things out. But none of them will be the reason I flee.

. . .

IT IS EIGHT-THIRTY on a frosty Monday morning. I'm in the kitchen, feeding Katie. I haven't had my coffee yet. The phone is ringing. I think about not answering it, but I'm too responsible. I set down her bowl and hurry into the living room.

I pick up the receiver. "Hello?"

"Good morning, darling," you say.

I look at the clock and do a quick calculation.

"It's five-thirty out there," I say, shivering in my bare feet. "What are you doing up so early?"

"I wanted to catch you before you went to work."

I reach for the throw on the back of the couch and wrap it around me. "So, how's it going?"

"I'm working my ass off. These guys are driving me crazy."

"Then you've seen the producers."

"Of course I've seen them. They want more rewrites. That's all they do is ask for more. But now I'm in real trouble, kid."

"Oh? What kind?"

"You've got to wire me five hundred dollars. Today."

"Why?"

"Because I owe it to the hotel and my guys won't pay."

"But you're working. They have to pay."

"Goddamn it! This is the way it goes out here. And I can't

ask them again. If I don't get this money, the whole project is fucked."

"But five hundred dollars. That's the last of my surgery money."

"Fuck the surgery money! I told you we'll get your god-damn teeth fixed. But in the meantime, I need that money. Now. Today. Do you understand me?"

I don't respond. I don't know what to do. I feel as though I'm being shoved back into a box with no air or light. I cannot think straight. I cannot breathe. I revert to pattern: What if he really needs the money? What if I'm being selfish? I can't live with myself if I become the reason he fails.

"Constance, are you listening?"

"Yeah."

"Go to Western Union and wire the money to me by noon. My time."

I shut my eyes. I flash on all the nights Mama and Daddy spent yelling at each other. I remember thinking, even as a child, Maybe Mama shouldn't be so hard on Daddy. And standing there in the cold morning light, the receiver to my ear, I tell myself, *She should have forgiven him. It would have been better for everybody.*

.   .   .

WITH MIKA by my side, I close my savings account. The teller counts out five one-hundred-dollar bills and says, "That didn't take long."

I think she means that it didn't take long for you to wipe out my account. It's not until I get back into the car that I realize she meant the transaction itself. She wasn't being mean, after all. I start to cry.

Mika holds me. He tells me not to worry. He says I can tell him anything. That he is a good listener.

"This was my surgery money," I sputter.

"Why are you giving it to him?"

"Because he says he has to have it."

Mika sets his jaw hard and looks out into the cold day. "What an asshole."

.   .   .

I CAN'T FIND Western Union. I thought I knew where one was in Tampa, but I was wrong. We stop at a pay phone on Dale Mabry. I am freezing. I don't own a good cold-weather jacket. The wind whips through the phone booth as if there were no walls. As I dial the number and ask for directions, Mika shields me with his body.

.   .   .

AFTER I WIRE THE MONEY, I find that I no longer feel any compunction to fret or cry. Indeed, I'm relieved to have no savings left. It means I have nothing left to pillage.

.   .   .

Two DAYS LATER, Mika stops by the office with a gift-wrapped package.

"Can I open it now?"

"Of course."

I tear away the paper. I gasp when I see what is inside.

"Oh my God. Oh my God. A typewriter!"

"You said you needed one."

"Thank you so much!"

He helps me pull it out of the box. It's lightweight and electric and peacock blue.

"This is the nicest thing anyone has ever done for me." I want to blabber on. I want to explain about the Selectric and it being off-limits and how I sneak behind your back to use it.

I want to say, "This typewriter helps me be independent."

But I do not say that word—*independent*—it's too complicated, and time is short, and life is becoming increasingly strange, like an exotic, delicious fruit tinged with arsenic.

. . .

AT A VEGETARIAN café in Tampa, Mika and I practice our new-found hobby: determinism. We try to fool ourselves into believing the future is something we can predict, even influence.

We plan dream houses on paper napkins. We talk about cities we'd like to explore. About children we may never have.

But we are shy determinists. None of these things we

speak of have any real flesh to them. It's as if we both privately fear that we don't have the courage to ensure that our lives will ever fully intersect.

And we are cautious—so, so cautious—expressing random desires, steering far clear of concrete details that might entangle us.

For instance, we never say, "One day you and I will walk down a cobblestoned road in Ravenna and cry in awe at the sight of the mosaics."

. . .

EVERY AFTERNOON for the next fourteen days, until you return home, the flower guy gains my front steps, knocks on the door, and hands me a bouquet of flowers.

I begin tipping him. I learn his name is Ed and that he attends St. Petersburg Junior College. He wants to be an engineer.

He says, "This dude must really have the hots for you."

"No. Not really. We're just good friends."

"Believe me," he says, "good friends don't send other friends flowers every day. I know. I'm in the business."

Whatever Mika's intentions may be, the result is that my living room resembles a greenhouse in full bloom. There is barely a space to set down so much as a key ring. I float among the flora, pausing to sniff the roses, reading the cards, adding fresh water. I try to choose which bouquets I will leave here and which ones I will take to my office. I am learning the names of flowers. Queen Anne's lace. Baby's breath. Bells of Ireland. I am becoming spoiled. Every hour of every day I want to be surrounded by blossoms.

Even Katie has noticed that the house is bustling with green living things. She looks around at daylilies, calla lilies, tulips, chrysanthemums, roses, and then glances up at me, her brow knitted in a little doggy frown, as if to say, "What now, Mama?"

.   .   .

I RARELY THINK ABOUT YOU.

It's not like in the old days when I would stare for hours out the window, praying for your return, blaming myself for your sins.

Lately, I've even allowed myself to believe the unthinkable: I want a different life.

The truth is, I'm beginning to resent you. And the resentment is spawning horrible realizations. Such as, I didn't want to sacrifice myself to Mama in her drunken old age. I don't want to sacrifice myself to yours.

But guilt and shame—they're real killers. Viruses of the soul. And as far as I can tell, nobody knows how to cure them.

.   .   .

I WANT TO BE a loyal, good person. I don't want to abandon you. On Judgment Day I don't want to hear God say, "You

thought your own paltry life was so important that you abandoned an old helpless man."

In short, I don't know how to leave.

.   .   .

I AM TRYING to spend more quality time with myself. This
means not running over to Heather and George's every spare
moment. And not making up work-related reasons to see
Mika. And not obsessing over what you may or may not be
doing. Or what Mika may or may not be doing. I am reading
again. I'm considering taking up a hobby. Gourmet cooking
would be good. And I can always bone up on my Spanish.

See, these things constitute plans. I've never had a plan
before. I just let life happen.

.   .   .

YOUR ABSENCE is teaching me things.

Alone, in a house full of flowers, I daydream a different
life, one born from the fair aspects of my past.

For instance, I remember my successes in school, how
my professors encouraged and even admired me. One called
me his protégée. They assumed my life would be filled with
music and art and creativity. They never imagined that I
would feel powerless to affect any positive change in my life.
Yes, I was their golden girl. I was the future they would never
have—their job was to teach me, my job was to ascend.

In this blessed solitude, manipulations, name-calling, beatings, and deceptions are not twenty-four-hour-a-day realities.

So, in your absence, I find the space to begin to think of myself in a new way.

And that is why your return is so devastating.

.   .   .

YOU COME HOME just before Christmas, bearing nothing but lies.

I know that now. I know there will never really be a movie. And that you won't ever find a job. I know you will drink yourself to death. I know you are not truly the man my mama wanted to marry. I know you are full of delusions fed by bitterness and liquor. I know something really awful: You are my Mama.

.   .   .

UNFORTUNATELY, your absence bred self-knowledge, but not much courage. So I am being a good girl.

Your first night back, I prepare a dinner of roast beef and carrots and potatoes. I even bake a chocolate cake. It is lopsided, but I'm convinced it will be tasty.

With a flick of your wrist, you push aside the fact that I gave your dog away. You have other things on your mind. You are drunk and are speaking at full volume. You call the producers in Hollywood nothing but a bunch of assholes.

I ask for details. Is the script finished? Did they like it? What happens next?

"Jesus, Constance. I worked really hard. Bunch of pricks. I showed them. I showed them what a real writer can do."

"So, they liked it?"

"Weeeee! They loved it!"

You get up from the table and start dancing around the room. You are smiling, glassy-eyed.

"Tell me about the flowers," you say.

"They're from a bunch of different people."

"Like who?"

"My publisher. And Heather and George. And Deidre and Phil. And some other people."

"And why, darling, would all those people send you flowers?"

"To celebrate. I've been doing a good job at the magazine, and they had a little party for me, and everybody was told to bring me flowers."

I feel as if I'm three years old, and Mama is catching me in a fib, and I fear I might wet myself.

You start laughing. "That's my girl!"

.   .   .

I LEAVE THE KITCHEN LIGHT ON so that the house won't be completely dark. With you home, shadows frighten me.

Your sleep is fitful. You yell out unintelligible curses. You punch the air.

I scoot over to the bed's edge. Katie gets between us and presses herself against me.

You slam the mattress with your fist. The room reeks of liquor. You stink of it. Your skin smells. The alcohol, once more, is giving off its stench through your pores.

I lay huddled against your darkness, realizing that my fear has gained a new dimension. I'm afraid of your death. This isn't to say I don't want you to die. I do. It would be the easiest solution. Like it was with Mama. Just die. Just go away because I'm not strong enough to do so myself.

But people don't just die. Especially drunks. They take their sweet time. And what's worse is that they take everyone with them, as far down as humanly possible. And when the muck and shit are so thick the world becomes an unmoveable object, the drunk escapes through death, and the living are left to stumble and wander through the wasteland the drunks created.

I ease out of bed, and Katie jumps silently to the floor. I tiptoe toward the door, but as I pass, you grab my arm and squeeze tight.

"Don't go," you whimper. "Please. I'm so scared."

This has been a long time coming. Nothing here is a surprise. I am Mama's daughter once more, ministering to the needs of a dying drunk. I know how to do this. I know how to stay up all night and press cold washcloths against a forehead feverish with night sweats. I know how to hold very still as the drunk hangs on, pleading for me to never leave. I know, come morning, how to behave. As if none of it ever happened.

· · ·

THREE HOURS LATER you are fully awake and ready for more.

"Get me a drink."

"I don't think you should have anything else. How about a Coke?"

"Give me a goddamn drink. Slut."

You violently grab at me, but I move away in time.

"Fine," I say, and in the dawning light I go to the kitchen and grab a jug of white wine from under the counter and a fresh glass.

When I return to the bedroom you are sitting up, holding your belly.

"Thank you, darling," you say. "I think I'm sick."

Your hands shake so violently that you spill the wine on the bed, but you seem not to notice.

"Then perhaps you ought to have something other than liquor."

"No! The wine will calm my stomach."

You take a big swig, lean back on your pillows, smooth the sheet, and then smile at me indulgently. "You look tired," you say in your radio voice. "Why don't you lie down for a while."

"I've got some things to do in the kitchen."

You shrug your shoulders. I back out of the room and close the door.

Katie is lying on the floor in the living room. As I walk in she beats her tail on the floor, *thump, thump,* and grins.

"Hi, little girly," I say. I walk over and rub her ears. I sit on the couch. She jumps up beside me. We curl up together and I close my eyes.

.   .   .

IN MY DREAM, you are as you exist in our waking hours: drunk and raging.

You lie in bed, calling me names.

I stand before you and plead for forgiveness. My teeth begin to drop out one by one and I don't know what is worse, the verbal harangue or my disappearing teeth.

Suddenly we are on all fours and you are raping me. I beg you to stop. You call me a cunt and grab me by my hair and begin pounding my head against the floor. I manage to turn over so that I can stare you in the eye as you kill me, but when I do, you transform yourself.

You become Mama. And now it's Mama in the bed, holding her big belly, begging me to never leave as I feed her white bread soaked in warm milk.

.   .   .

YOU HAVE THE D.T.'S. You shake and vomit and ramble about God and your sons and your worthless father and your whore of a mother. You speak of your parents as if they are in the room with us, as if they haven't been dead for thirty-some years. I cannot imagine Hell being a worse place than this.

I consider throwing out all the liquor in the house, but I know what you would do. You'd get into your slick silver Audi and buy some more, or sit in a bar until you pass out, or get behind the wheel and kill somebody. No, it's best if you stay home and do your drinking.

You have made a horrible mess in the bathroom. I pull on my rubber gloves and hold my breath as I clean your vomit. I wonder how long a person can live by breathing only through their mouth?

I fix you white bread in warm milk. You tell me to melt some butter in it. I do. You eat it greedily. Milk runs down your chin.

You say, "Thank you, darling. I don't know what I would do without you."

Ten minutes later, as you doze, you shit on yourself. I clean it up. I help you into the bathroom and rub the soapy washcloth against the fat white skin of your ass.

.　.　.

THE NIGHTMARES do not cease. Each time I fall asleep, you become Mama and she becomes you. Your hatred bleeds into hers. I cannot tell one rage from the other.

.　.　.

MIKA AND I do not see each other very often. We talk on the phone. He comes to the office. We work. We are learning about each other. We are becoming friends. But the physical stuff is on hold.

I can't allow myself to be touched right now. I can't be loved.

. . .

ON CHRISTMAS DAY I visit my sister. You visit your sons.

This is a good arrangement. I need time away. I need to practice living a normal life.

I help my sister bake a ham. I play with my nephew. We open presents.

Deidre asks how I got the bruise on my arm. I say, I don't remember. I can't explain how I got a bruise that resembles a large hand. Nothing else, nothing I can think of, makes an imprint like that.

She doesn't suspect. She says, "I know, I got this bruise the other day on my thigh, and for the life of me I don't remember doing it. I must have hit the corner of my desk at school or something."

I wonder if I said, "Look at this mark on my breast. This is from being held down in the middle of the night—woken up from a haunted sleep—and a lit cigarette being stubbed out on my skin," if she would then say, "Ow! That must have hurt. Look at this mole. My bra strap keeps rubbing against it. I think I might have it removed."

Actually, this conversation with my sister is like all the conversations we've ever had. We never get to the truth. We glide on the surface, afraid.

I watch her fix her Christmas dinner plate. She is solemn, focused. I can only imagine what this must be like for her, decisions about food.

My sister says she weighs ninety-seven pounds. I don't believe her. I'm not even sure if she hits ninety.

I have a theory about Deidre's anorexia. I think its seeds were planted years ago, during those god-awful nights our parents fought. And the beatings and name-calling we suffered at the hands of our mama, they watered those seeds, made them plump and healthy. And the excruciating hours Deidre spent by Mama's deathbed gave the seeds the strength to poke their first, evil tendrils up through the dirt of our lives. And Mama's death? Sun and rain.

Yes, I spiraled into a depression that lasted for years—it still clings to me. But Deidre simply stopped eating. Six months after Sean was born, Deidre's weight had plummeted to sixty-eight pounds. Phil and I Baker-Acted her. We got her admitted into St. Joseph's, the same hospital where Mama died. Every afternoon we would put Sean in Phil's big red truck and park outside the hospital at the appointed time. We'd stand there, waiting for her to appear—she was always there within seconds—and then we'd hold Sean up for her to see him. She'd stand at her seventh-floor window in her nightgown, looking like a walking skeleton, and she'd smile and wave at her baby.

We'd say, "Look, Sean, wave at Mama. There she is. That's your Mama."

We did this every day for thirty days.

Those people at the hospital. They did not cure her.

I watch her now, studying the bowl of green beans. She puts three on her plate. She slices a piece of ham the size of her pinky finger. Phil doesn't seem to notice. I'm sure he's used to it, that living and loving a woman who barely allows herself the most minimal nutrition is simply the way things are in this house. He used to challenge her, but Deidre can have an acid tongue when she feels cornered. And anorexics are ingenious at devising strategies to avoid eating. Maybe he decided that a direct approach was simply too debilitating. For both of them. But me, I don't care. Deidre and I have always had our sisterly skirmishes. And besides, I have to do something. So I take her on, even though it's Christmas.

"Deidre, you have to eat more than that," I say.

She rolls her eyes. "I'm already stuffed!"

"How can you be stuffed? You haven't eaten anything."

"I've picked!"

I looked up my sister's name in a dictionary a few years ago. I love her name. It is so lyrical. So unlike *Constance*, which sounds severe and ungiving. I used the Irish spelling *Deirdre*, which is what the priests always called her, letting that first *r* roll off their tongues in a sparkling brogue. But the Deirdre I discovered in the dictionary was far from sparkling. According to Irish legend, she was raised to be the bride of the king of Ulster. Instead, when the time came for her to be married, she eloped with her true love. The king, incensed, killed her lover. And Deirdre, consumed with grief, committed suicide, her death bringing chaos and ruin to Ireland, as had been prophesied. In 1910, John Millington Synge wrote a play about this Deirdre. He named it *Deirdre of the Sorrows*.

I have never told her about her name. The sadness embedded in that story is too close to the bone. I think it would hurt her, maybe even haunt her.

Or perhaps she knows. Perhaps the story of a beloved, beautiful princess meeting a tragic fate resonates deep inside her starved soul.

"Please, Deidre," I say, "at least eat some salad."

.   .   .

AT TWILIGHT I leave my sister's house. I take the Gandy Bridge into St. Pete. I say to no one in particular, "Thank you," when I pull up in front of my place and see that your car is not there.

I go inside and greet Katie. I fix her a bowl of food and chop into it ham I've brought from Deidre's. Then I check the answering machine. It is your son, wishing you and us a merry Christmas.

You're not even a good liar, I think. You almost always get caught.

. . .

New Year's Eve day, without explanation, you leave the house around 9:00 a.m. I call Heather and George, and they invite me over for lunch.

"Mika will be here," Heather says. "I just thought you should know."

I'm grateful for the information. It means I won't show up in rumpled clothes and no makeup.

. . .

I'm sitting on Heather and George's couch, sipping tea, trying to appear nonplussed when Mika walks in.

There are greetings all around, but I'm the only one he kisses. He sits beside me and takes my hand and asks if I'm okay.

Before I can answer, Heather and George slip out of the room. Suddenly there is much work to be done in the kitchen.

Mika and I kiss and kiss. Over and over.

"I have missed you."

"I missed you, too."

"I want you to know something. After the holidays, I'm filing for divorce."

"You don't have to. Don't do it for me." I think I'm going to cry. I don't want his life to fall apart.

He holds my hands tenderly, as if they are precious. He looks beyond us, at the floor or bookshelf, I'm not sure, and says slowly, in the same way a cautious person places one foot precisely in front of the other, "I need to change my life. My marriage has been dead for a long time. She knows that. I know that."

Then he looks at me and touches my cheek. "I don't know what is going to happen. But I know I want to know you better. I think we've got to try to be together."

I'm scared that he is lying and that if he knows me better he will discover that I am a woman unsuited for love. Maybe I will somehow wreck his life. Maybe whatever curse boils through my bones will destroy us. Maybe I'm incapable of leaving a dying, battering drunk.

"I want things to work out, Mika. I want us both to be happy. But I'm not safe right now. I can't really explain. But I need some time."

Mika, of course, presses me. He wants to know what I mean by not being safe.

"I want to help you, Connie. Please. Let me help."

I don't know where my next words come from, or why I suddenly feel strong enough to look Mika in the eyes without flinching from that old fear that I'm no damn good, or why at this particular moment I choose to speak the first truly honest sentence in my life. But out it comes. And it's so simple, like ice. "You can't help me, Mika. Not right now. Nobody can."

. . .

I DRIVE HOME from Heather and George's while it's still light out. I do not want to walk into a dark house.

As I wait at a red light, I have this thought: *There is not a chance in hell that I will leave you because of Mika. If I leave, it will be because I am a strong, talented person with potential. And you steal those things from me.*

So how do I get out?

. . .

IF I AM LUCKY, you will not come home tonight. You will spend New Year's Eve with a woman closer to your own age. She will rub your thin hair, and then try to blow you, and you will both giggle and have another drink.

I come into the house and drop my purse and pet my dog. I go into the kitchen and throw open the fridge. I just want some cold water. That's all. But I never get that far. My gaze doesn't get past the objects placed with clinical precision on the second shelf. A vial filled with clear fluid and a syringe.

As promised, our friend with multiple sclerosis has given you a grandiose gift—a dose of his hard-on medicine. You must have said something to him such as, "If I can just fuck her, then she'll leave that goddamn photographer alone."

Throw it away. Get back in the car and find one of those giant Dumpsters behind a business and toss it in. I reach for it but then reconsider. If I throw it out, you will beat me senseless. This is what my instinct tells me.

Perhaps this is your idea of a joke. And even if it isn't, won't I have time to grab my keys and Katie and head out the door before you come after me? I mean, you've got to inject yourself in that place, in your dick.

You don't have the nerve.

.   .   .

I NEED TO GET OUT OF HERE. But where do I go? It's New Year's Eve. Everyone is busy. Everyone is partying. Heather and George have plans. Deidre and Phil have plans. Mika is a married man. Just bunker in.

You probably won't be home until daybreak. Maybe not even then.

Better safe than sorry, though. In case I need to make a quick exit, I set my purse, keys, and Katie's leash on the desk in the sunroom next to the front door.

From the kitchen I retrieve a bag of potato chips and a Diet Coke. Katie follows me into the bedroom, where I latch the hook on the bedroom door. *Just in case, just in case.*

We pile into bed and I turn on the TV. I think, *This is pitiful. I am young and have all my limbs and a decent enough number of brain cells, and the best I can manage on New Year's Eve is Guy Lombardo.*

Katie snuggles beside me. I scratch her belly and channel surf. I feed her chips. Eventually, she falls asleep. She snores. I keep my hand on her rising and falling chest. I watch the red ball. I listen to the happy drunks in Times Square shout, "Happy New Year!"

Maybe what I don't understand about life is everyone is a fake, and we're all secretly miserable.

I turn off the TV and close my eyes.

.   .   .

ONCE AGAIN, you invade my dreams. You are lying on Mama's couch. Your belly is distended and the whites of your eyes are yellow. I look closer and see that the couch is made of booze bottles.

You beg, "Please, help me."

"What do you need? What can I do?"

"Come here, baby. I need you. I need you."

You pull me down so near that all I can see are your rotting teeth. And I hear Mama's voice.

She says—no, you say, "Go to hell."

.   .   .

I WAKE TO the sound of Katie barking. This is her low, guttural don't-mess-with-me bark.

From somewhere in the house you yell, "Where are you, Constance! I'm going to fuck you! Fuck you so hard you won't be able to walk!"

I hear you stumble over a table or a chair. It bangs to the floor.

"Goddamn it!"

You throw something at the bedroom door. You try the doorknob, and when that doesn't work, you begin pounding.

"Let me in! Unlock the goddamn door!"

I cannot move. I cower in bed, unable to gather my wits.

You kick the door. I watch the wood give. It bows. I have underestimated your strength. You *can* kick this door in. Without a doubt. In fact, you are going to kick it in, and then you are going to rape me.

I scramble out of bed and run over to the chest of drawers. It is heavy with your extensive wardrobe, and I find myself suddenly grateful that you're a clotheshorse. I get behind the dresser and push as hard as I can. The latch is one or two blows away from giving. I grunt, expelling all my breath, as the chest moves one, two, three feet. That's all I need to block the door.

But you are still kicking and cursing and threatening to fuck me. I fear the chest of drawers isn't heavy enough. I get on my side of the bed and manage to push the mattress off the box spring and tilt it against the chest. I look around the room. What else, what else? I unplug the TV. "You whore, I'm going to give you what you've been wanting!" I manage to lift the TV off its stand. I grunt and stumble under the weight. A few inches from the floor, I lose my grip and drop it. I push it against the upended mattress. Your blows are becoming less intense, but I keep piling on objects anyway: shoes, side tables, an old comforter (it's kind of heavy). I pause for one second, and think, Maybe I should flee now. Out the French doors and off the porch and into the New Year.

But I am afraid. You have become to me the Boogie Man. Maybe that is your plan.

In the midst of this hell, suddenly there is silence. No more cursing. No more pounding. No more furniture or glass being hurled at the locked door.

I don't know where you are. Maybe you are waiting for me on the porch. You can read my mind. You know everything. I stumble over the box spring and make certain the French doors are locked.

And then Katie and I huddle on the floor on the far side of the bed. She is at full alert. Her ears are pricked, the hair on her back ridged. Now and again she growls. We sit together for a long time, listening. We hear you fumbling through the night, sometimes cursing and other times carrying on unintelligible conversations with imaginary demons. I don't know how long you go on like this. It feels as if you rage for hours. And I am so grateful when finally, finally, you exhaust yourself. I hear you flop on the couch. And then I hear nothing more.

Katie, sensing the danger has passed, closes her eyes. She sleeps.

I hang on to her. This dog is my life preserver. I lie down beside her. Her nose is wet and cold against my neck. I should be shattered. But I'm not. I am an idiot savant. I know only one thing in all the world, and I know this with a clarity that is divine: When Katie wakes, the night will have vanished. And we will leave.

. . .

As is her habit, when day breaks, Katie wakes me by licking my face. I rub behind her ears. "You're Mama's good girl. Yes, you are," I whisper.

The house remains silent. I feel sure that you are deep in the grips of one of your comalike sleeps.

Quickly, I gather up some clothes. I don't own any luggage, so I take the pillow slip off my pillow and stuff it with a few pairs of jeans, T-shirts, and some makeup. I unlock the French doors. I grab Katie's leash and attach it to her collar.

On January 1, 1986, with purse, keys, pillow slip, and dog in hand, I leave.

. . .

I do not know where to go. Someplace where you cannot find me. That means friends and family are out of the question.

So I just drive.

I think about my mama, about how she would get in the car and wander around Jacksonville Beach. Sometimes we would go to the restaurant at the pier. I was a little kid, not even in school, and it would be a cold north Florida day, and we'd walk out to the restaurant in the whipping, nor'easter wind. And I always imagined that the wind would lift me up, and I'd fly over Jacksonville Beach. In my fantasy, Mama would say, "There goes Connie!" And people would come out of their shops and homes and stare up at me. Dogs would bark. I would wave. People would scratch their heads in wonder. And I'd hear their voices. "She sure is something!" they would say. And when I set my feet back on this earth, everyone would be nice to me.

But what would really happen is this. Mama and I would step into the restaurant and the lady behind the counter—the one with her hair done up in a bun and the Dracula red lips—would say, "Hello, Lee, sure is cold today."

Mama would respond, "Burrrrr! You can say that again."

Then we would sit at a table overlooking the water, and Mama would drink coffee and smoke cigarettes and stare into space, listening to the waves crash against the shore. I would eat a fried-grouper sandwich with extra tartar sauce. I'd usually get potato chips rather than fries, and I always ate my pickle spear. I would drink a Dr Pepper. Mama said they were good for me. And I was kind of happy for a while and Mama was quiet. It was just us and the surf.

Maybe it is this memory that causes me to drive west, toward water.

"Once we leave here, we'll never hear the sound of the surf again."

I drive all the way to the Gulf of Mexico and a little town

named Indian Pass. I stop at a convenience store and buy a package of Fig Newtons, a jar of instant coffee, some artificial creamer, and two cans of dog food. I get back in the car and drive slowly along the beach road, looking for a spot that will suit my needs. I am surprised at how little traffic there is, this being winter and snowbird season. I guess people tend to spend the holidays at home.

About a mile down on the Gulf side I spy a small, nondescript motel. EFFICIENCY ROOMS, VACANCY, CLEAN. I like it. Nothing fancy. Basic. Lots of sea grapes growing out front. Katie may be a problem, but I'll give it a try.

Act calm and polite, I tell myself as I open the door to the motel office. No one is around but there is a bell on the counter. I can hear the TV blaring in the back room.

"Hello!" No one responds. I ring the bell. That does the trick.

Out comes the owner, a silver-haired, blue-eyed old woman, who reminds me of Mrs. Harris and her braces.

"We don't get very many people checking in on New Year's Day," she says.

"Well, you know, you've got to take vacations when you can." I try to sound upbeat. I don't want to give myself away. No one can know that I'm on the run.

Everything goes fine until we get to the topic of Katie.

"No pets," she says firmly.

"But she is housebroken and really well behaved."

"I'm sorry, but it's our policy."

"Would you just come out and meet her? She's really a nice dog."

To my astonishment, the woman does as I ask. She stands with lips pursed as I open the passenger door. Katie leaps out and wags her tail and smiles up at the old woman.

"Oh my goodness! She's smiling!" The lady offers Katie her hand, and Katie licks it. "I do love dogs." She straightens up. "Okay, we'll try it. But if she starts barking, I'll have to ask you to leave."

As we follow her back into the office she says, shaking her head, "My husband is going to kill me!"

. . .

THE ROOM IS PERFECT. I am used to small spaces. A single bed. A compact, two-burner stove and an oven so small it reminds me of the Easy Bake Oven I played with when I was five. The bathroom has a shower but no tub. That's okay. Who needs a tub when you're at the beach? The floor is made of terrazzo, so it is hard and cold and extremely clean. A small TV sits on a bamboo stand. Through the single window I can look out at the parking lot, a high-rise condo, and a slice of the Gulf.

My brain is buzzing—a low, dull buzz—as if it's full of lint. I should try to take a nap. This is a safe space. There is no reason for me not to sleep.

I pull back the covers, sit on the edge of the bed, wipe off my feet, and lie down. The sheets are white and bleached. They feel cool, welcoming. Katie jumps up and snuggles beside me. Good girl, Katie, good girl. I close my eyes. They hurt. It's as if the inside of my lids are lined with sandpaper. An image blooms: Katie and I huddled beside the bed, the door creaking on its hinges, the latch hook shimmying out of the wood frame, the door panels bowing. Filthy, filthy, filthy—that's what I am. From the inside out. White trash trying to pass. Who do you think you are, you no good useless child!

I want everything to stop. I don't know what this means. Do I want to die? Or do I want to be somebody new? Do I want to reinvent myself so that the hateful voices in my head are silenced? Change my name? Dye my hair? Move to Bombay or Miami?

My stomach flip-flops. I'm going to be sick. I rush from the bed into the bathroom and flip up the toilet lid. I have not eaten, so it is dry heaves that rattle me. My muscles and ribs contort under their force. My belly contracts and expands as if a demon is down there, punching and pulling.

But I am so glad that I'm not truly vomiting. I would have to clean up the mess. I'd probably get kicked out. And then what?

Slowly, the contractions ease. I stand and support myself by holding on to the wall. I flip back the shower curtain and turn on the water. When it is close to scalding, I get in. I never want to be touched again.

. . .

I SLEEP. Nightmares come and go, but they do not stir me awake. I take them for granted.

So, this is life.

. . .

THE SOUND OF A CAR DOOR slamming and Katie barking wakes me.

"No, no, baby, no barking. Shhh, Katie, shhh." I pull her to me and rub her chest and belly. "You are such a good girl."

I look at the clock. Four-fifteen. I have slept away the day.

"We've got to get up, Miss Katie. Yes, we do."

I kick the covers off and rub the sleepers out of my eyes. I go into the bathroom and pee. Katie follows me. I rub her head while I empty my bladder.

"Hey, little girly, I bet you need to go out, don't you?"

The buzzing in my head has stopped, but I possess no more energy than I did before my nap. In fact, I feel as if I've been drugged, as if poison is coursing through my veins, thickening my blood, blunting my perceptions.

I flush and then go into the other room, looking for the motel room key and Katie's leash. I find them both under the pillow case which I had tossed onto the floor.

A walk, that is what we both need.

· · ·

THE WIND OFF the Gulf is cold and brisk. Foam ghosts circle our legs and scatter amid the lapping waves. Katie chases them and, I think, is confused when at her touch they disappear.

· · ·

BACK IN THE ROOM, I drink instant coffee and watch the evening news. Dan Rather gives a global breakdown of New Year's celebrations across the globe. During the break, they run commercials for constipation, hemorrhoids, and cars. When Dan returns, they run footage of war in the Middle East and famine in Africa. I break out the Fig Newtons and share them with Katie. She swallows hers nearly whole. I nibble off the sweet bread coating and eat the filling separately. The news broadcast closes with a feel-good feature about people who work through the holidays so that the rest of us can be safe, happy, and entertained: firemen, long-distance phone operators, football players.

I think, I don't feel sorry for any of them. Especially the football players. One of the athletes actually says, "It's a sacrifice we have to make for our fans."

"Fuck you," I say to the TV, and then I eat another Fig Newton.

. . .

As I drift to sleep, I experience a surprisingly comforting thought: No one on the planet knows where I am.

. . .

I could live here. That's what I think as morning dawns. It is January 2. The second day of the new year. I don't need much in my life. Katie, my books, and simple food. Homeless people survive on less. It would be an ascetic existence. Which is fine. I've never been into material things. You can't be if you don't have any money. And when I was little, didn't I want with all my heart to become a nun, to wear that crisp, severe habit and lead a holy life? Maybe I could do that. I could join a convent. No. They wouldn't let me keep Katie. That wouldn't work. And remember what they did to Audrey Hepburn in *The Nun's Story*. They cut off all her hair. And they did it in a brutish fashion, too. No style whatsoever. This place is sixty-five dollars a night. Maybe they could give me a monthly rate. I could say to people, "I live out at the beach."

. . .

This morning I found a little neighborhood grocery store. I bought Katie a bag of chew bones and me a can of cheese ravioli. Ravioli is one of my favorite foods on the planet. I haven't had it in years. I wonder if I'll still like it. Also,

I bought some sweet rolls. I can dunk them in my instant coffee.

.   .   .

IF I STAY HERE, I'll get rid of the hokey motel art. I'll just give it back to the lady who runs the place. She can use it in another room.

They're really going to have to come down on the rent, though. Sixty-five dollars times thirty. Jesus! That's almost two thousand dollars!

I guess I'm going to have to think about this.

.   .   .

AN AMAZING THING HAPPENS. I fall into a full-bodied, nothing-else-in-the-world-exists nap, and I do not suffer nightmares. Instead, I dream about Miss Vivian.

Oh my God, Miss Vivian! That was so long ago.

I am a little girl, and Mama is gone. Don't know where to. Miss Vivian comes over to take care of me. She smells of lilacs. Her skin is the color of dark cocoa. She is wearing a dress with flowers on it. Her hair is long for a black person. It is straight and coarse and flips at her shoulders. She is a pretty lady.

She smiles when she sees me. I run to her. I throw myself into her opened arms. She hugs me tight. "You are such a good little girl," she says. "I have missed you so much!"

. . .

I WAKE FROM this dream, happy. Miss Vivian was in my life for the shortest time. She was simply a lady who lived down the road. That's all. But she was kind to me. For—what was it?—a few months, maybe a year, there was somebody in my life who told me I was a good little girl and that she loved me. She never seemed to expect anything in return.

Maybe she is the reason I'm not in jail. Or on drugs. Or dead. Maybe that pathetic hopefulness I always lecture myself about is actually a good thing. Maybe it springs from these deep-seated memories of a time when I was loved.

. . .

MY DOG IS RESTLESS. There isn't any place for her to look out. And I keep telling her to be quiet. The whole motel thing is starting to wear on us both.

She eats her dinner and part of mine.

Then we walk on the beach for about an hour. I try to have profound thoughts. With the surf pounding and the waves breaking, profundity shouldn't be a problem. But all I come up with is this: I'm fucked. I have no place to live. No money. No resources. But at least I have my car. That's a start.

Katie and I return to the room. I take her into the bathroom and wipe the sand off her paws. She licks my face. I hug her. I wonder if she realizes that we are homeless, and that I don't feel capable of decision making, and that time is running out.

"Maybe you need a new mama," I say as I wipe sand away from below her eye. For a few seconds I imagine a better life for her. A sodded yard and children to play with and a big house with her own bed and a matching collar and leash. I can run an ad in the paper, and I can interview applicants, and when I find the perfect family I will adopt her out. I will be happy for her. I will not cry. I will think, finally she has a good life. And then I will be free, truly free: no home, no dog, no responsibilities, no one to care for, no one to look out for but me.

. . .

I WAKE TO THE SOUND of Katie crying. She is burrowing under the covers and pressing herself hard against me. Lightning glazes the room. Thunder reverberates off the Gulf and echoes over land. Thunder has always terrified Katie.

"It's okay, baby, it's okay." I hold her and try to comfort her.

The wind is pushing the rain vertically. I can tell by the sound it makes as it hits the window. I reach for the clock and bring it close. It is 3:30 A.M.

Happy birthday, I say to myself. January 3. I have just turned twenty-seven years old, and I have run away from home, fled a violent man, and am huddled in a motel room with my dog, my whereabouts a mystery to everyone. Try as I might, I bear no guilt over having run away, possibly causing the few people in this world who care about me to worry. At this juncture in my life, other people's needs cannot affect me. My world is centered on surviving, on me and Katie figuring out our next move. Everyone and everything else is on hold. If and when I resurface, the people who love me will just have to understand.

And none of this is so bad, I think. I mean, what is really wrong?

. . .

I FEED KATIE Alpo and eat my sweet roll and drink my weak instant coffee and try to come up with a plan. I could go back. I could just waltz in and say breezily, "Hi," and offer no explanation and start all over again as if nothing wrong ever happened.

Just the thought makes me sick.

. . .

KATIE AND I walk the beach. She loves everything about this place except the water. She hates to get her paws wet. So I work hard at steering her clear of the waves.

I wonder what you are thinking. Have you called my sister? Heather and George? Anyone at the magazine? Are you worried? Do you care at all?

Fuck you.

Maybe Mika has left his wife.

Maybe I will find a million dollars lying in an abandoned wallet on the beach.

Maybe I will go back to the room and look in the mirror and say to my reflection, "I am not to blame. This is not my fault."

. . .

IT'S NOT JUST the violence. It's the whole package.

I'm tired of you having power over me.

Who are you to say who I can be friends with? Who I should hire or fire? Or how I should wear my hair? Or what I'm supposed to be when I grow up?

I'm sick of you.

. . .

I NEED TO TAKE a shower and put on clean clothes. I need to brush my teeth and fluff my hair. I need to feel good about myself. It is my birthday, after all.

. . .

KATIE AND I sit on the sand. She watches seagulls and lunges at them when they venture too near.

I watch the Gulf. The waves unfurl. Endlessly.

Maybe that's why Mama no longer wanted to live by the ocean—the noise had begun to haunt her. Maybe she heard the voices of her past rise from the sea mist, voices that bemoaned her family's ancient, unbroken chain of violence. By fleeing, perhaps she was trying to slip away from the past, escape its sorrows, and avoid the echo of its sins. *"You will never hear the surf again."* Maybe it wasn't a statement but a prayer.

How odd it is that she could never sustain her recognition and rejection of our curse. How ironic that the harder she tried, the deeper she plunged. Mama never surfaced.

I hold Katie closer, shut my eyes, and listen to the surf song. In its infinite whisper, I find only comfort.

With Katie by my side, I rise to my feet and gaze out at the horizon. For the first time in years, I feel as though I can breathe.

.   .   .

WHY DIDN'T I LEAVE SOONER? Why did I stick around at all? The first time you ever raised your voice or lifted a fist, why didn't I kick your stinking ass out?

The answers aren't easy. And right now, in my current condition, I can't grasp many of them at all. But I know that in the next few weeks, months, probably even years, the answers will come. Some will be complex, others shameful. Almost all of them will certainly be born from my past.

. . .

I wanted to please Mama.

I wanted a daddy.

I wanted to help you.

How could I have turned you away? That would have been like spitting on my parents' graves.

I didn't want to be a bad person.

Once I was in, there was no easy escape. I was already fragile. But you made me insane. You with your beatings and slurs and shenanigans—all of it worked on me, preventing me from making rational decisions. I could not even perceive that I had choices.

. . .

I will not beat myself up over not leaving you sooner. I will be sad that I didn't find my way out until it was nearly too late, but I will not blame myself. Yes, I was always leaving you. But I needed some things in place. I needed a good job. I needed friends who could act as my safety net. Yes, friends. They are so important. Heather and George and Mika—with them I temporarily pushed aside my sorrow. I laughed. I learned. I dreamed.

Did they know they were helping me? Did they realize that just through their small acts of kindness I was able to feel for the first time in many years that perhaps I had a right to be on this earth? That I was worthy?

. . .

WHAT DOES KATIE KNOW?

. . .

SHE KEPT ME SAFE. How does one repay the loyalty, the goodness, the love of a dog?

. . .

WE CHECK OUT of the motel at noon. We drive through the beach neighborhoods. There are many fine houses here. Good landscaping (all very tropical) and basketball hoops attached to turquoise walls and professionally made signs neatly hung from painted wooden posts announcing the names of the homes. THE DOLPHIN WATCH. THE SEA VIEW. THE GULF WIND. If I lived here I would have a sense of humor. I would name my house THE SAND SPUR PALACE. But I would not have any lighthouse or pipe-smoking sea captain lawn ornaments cluttering my yard.

As I drive across the bridge onto the mainland, I make a

mental inventory of my possessions. I have my dog and my car and twenty bucks in my purse.

It could be worse.

.　　.　　.

I DON'T TELL Heather very much. I don't need to. She has a sixth sense about things. Which at this moment I am very grateful for. I cannot yet confess my sins. I just need a place to stay. That's it. Nothing more. Until I get things figured out.

They have many cats so Katie cannot stay with me. I call my sister. She doesn't seem to mind.

"When are you bringing her over?"

"Now."

.　　.　　.

I HATE BEING AWAY from Katie for even a few days. But I am so grateful to my sister for taking care of her. And maybe Katie will charm Deidre. Maybe they'll become friends. I bet they do.

.　　.　　.

WAS IT ALWAYS this simple? Did all I ever need to do was tell one person, ask one solitary soul for a little help?

.　.　.

SITTING IN THE DARK, in Heather and George's living room, while they sleep, I tell Mika everything. I confess everything. He holds me. He cries with me. He kisses my forehead and my cheek and my hands. "You are so good, Connie," he says. "No one should ever hurt you."

.　.　.

HEATHER PUTS ME in the car and drives me around and together we find an apartment for me to move into.

I am fragile. She isn't. She negotiates a price and a move-in date and various other details I can't really grasp.

With her help, what once seemed monumental, beyond my reach, becomes a simple errand accomplished within the space of a single afternoon.

.　.　.

YOU FIND ME at their apartment. You stand in the street below and scream.

"Call the police," I say.

"No, let me go talk to him."

George is calm. He believes in nonviolence and in the basic decency of all people. But he doesn't know you.

.　.　.

KATIE AND I have moved into a duplex one block from the bay.

Out front there's a giant saguaro cactus (taller than the house) and terrazzo floors. It is simply furnished. It is clean. And full of light.

I have a phone and electricity and water. I wander from room to room, looking. I turn lamps on. I run water. I open the freezer and gaze in.

Can you believe it! I am on my own.

Discoveries abound.

For instance, I never knew before yesterday that I like the taste of basil.

I know this sounds like no big deal. But believe you me, it's a sign. Like a baby crawling.

. . .

ALL OF MY BELONGINGS are still at the house. I've considered letting you keep everything. But you don't own me anymore. And you surely don't deserve my possessions, no matter how meager they may be.

. . .

I AM NOT FOOLISH enough to go alone. So I ask Mika to help me.

. . .

WE DO NOT KNOW where you are or when you might return. So we work quickly.

First we go after items I can't replace: my typewriter, books, photo albums, awards. Then it's on to clothes, hot curlers, dishes.

I am in the kitchen, wrestling pots and pans. Mika is ferrying a box of books out to his car.

I am on my hands and knees, reaching for a cookie sheet in the bottom cabinet when I hear you yell, "She's back here!" I scramble to my feet and look out the kitchen window.

You have parked on the side street, toward the rear of the house. You are running toward the kitchen. And your son is right behind you.

I start to yell, "Mika!" but before I can, you and/or your son kick in the back door. Insanely—or perhaps out of habit—I run into the bedroom and latch the door.

What am I going to do? Get out. Get out now! Fuck! My tapes! I forgot about my minicassettes. All my interviews. All my hard work. I can't leave without them.

I run into the sunroom and sweep the tapes into the only thing I can find, a wastebasket.

Mika steps onto the porch.

"They're here!" I scream, searching the drawer for more tapes. "Start the car!"

"Let's go!" He reaches for me just as you bust down the bedroom door.

We flee down the steps and into Mika's car. I'm holding

the wastebasket tight. To me, just like Mika's gift of the type-writer, the tapes symbolize independence, intellectual and otherwise.

Mika's tires squeal as he guns the engine. We fly down the road. You are right behind us. Your son, the deputy, knows how to drive fast and what chances to take. You are on our bumper, trying to force us to pull over. You wrapped in the silver skin of your Audi, and your son in civilian clothes—as far as onlookers can tell, we're just four jerks hot-rodding through city streets.

What do you want? What would you do if you caught us? Would you beat us? Shoot us? Slit our throats? Is exerting power over me that important to you?

Mika runs red lights and stop signs. Drivers honk and give us the finger. Pedestrians jump back onto sidewalks. We are going to die. We head the wrong way down a one-way street. Mika takes a curve so fast and tight I'm sure we are about to flip. Then he heads into the maze that is the St. Pete marina.

I look over my shoulder. I see only water and sailboats and a young woman walking a dog and beyond the geometric shapes of the buildings that comprise downtown.

But these observations are not important. At this moment, there is only one piece of information in my universe that matters, that cannot be changed, reversed, unbound: I do not see you.

.   .   .

THIS IS A permanent state of affairs.

I will never lay eyes on you again.

You will never hurt me.

Not physically.

Not mentally.

Occasionally you will enter my dreams, but that's a fair trade-off.

Because when I wake I remember who I am.

Epilogue

THIS IS WHAT YOU DO NOT KNOW.

Despite your systematic ransacking of my savings, I finally got my surgery.

I was on the table for seven hours. My bones, the surgeon said, were so hard the saw blade barely cut through them. When I learned this, I thought of my mama. She always accused me of being the hard head in the family. I guess she was right about some things.

The surgeon moved my jaw forward one full inch and then screwed the pieces together with steel plates and bolts. He decided against the prosthetic chin.

I remained in ICU for four days.

Mika never left my side.

He also would not allow me to look in a mirror. No one would.

The day after my surgery, I realized something was protruding beyond the tip of my nose. Thanks to the tubes and the wiring shut of my jaws and the splint in my mouth, I could not speak or even grunt. So I kept pointing at my face. Mika finally understood what I was asking.

"Your lips are swollen," he explained.

A nurse slathered them three times a day with Preparation H.

In total, it took the doctors five years to fix my face. And when the ordeal was over, when I looked normal, when no one could any longer dismiss me at a glance due to my physical appearance, in my mind I was still that little kid with the buckteeth whose classmates had made fun of her. I was still that tortured teenager whose mother screamed at her to push harder on those front teeth. In this way, I remained the frightened young woman who never questioned the sanity of your cruelty.

So it took longer, maybe seven or eight years, before the perfectly fine face staring back at me in the mirror replaced the shy and ashamed girl who had lived life fearfully for nearly thirty years.

Listen to me: I have learned to appreciate my new face. But more importantly, I have also learned to love the old one. That kid, she wasn't so bad. She didn't deserve to be beaten. Not by Mama. Not by you. Not by anyone.

But I'm not finished yet. There is still more you don't know.

Mika not only never left me through my hard days of postsurgery. He never left me. Period. He is my partner in life. He is my wholeness. He does not hit me or yell at me. He does not call me names. He whispers away my nightmares. Sure, we have our rough times, but we are committed to honoring the goodness in each other. And I am profoundly grateful that the man I married knew me presurgery. It means he cherishes all of me—both my faces—the old and the new.

You need to understand this: Mika and I are good together. We create books and art and gardens. We raise dogs. We love.

After we married we left Florida for Kansas. It's not important that you know anything about our time in Kansas other than this: One day I was home alone (Mika was at work and the new semester at the University of Kansas had not yet begun) and I received a phone call from an editor I'd worked with in Tampa. She was double-checking facts from an interview I had done for her right before I left town. She asked if I still had my notes.

"Better than that, I have my tapes."

A light snow had started to fall. Katie was lying by my feet. She loved the snow. "I'll take you out, girly, right after I find this tape." She thumped her tail twice, as was her habit, and went back to sleep.

I popped three tapes into my player before the past rose palpably like a surreal genie who insists on laying bare the truth.

My study in our rented house in Lawrence, Kansas, was

suddenly filled with the sound of your voice. Katie stood and
began to pace. She whined. I petted her head. I listened once,
but did not trust what I heard. I rewound the tape and listened again.

Why you recorded yourself in this particular circumstance I will never know. Perhaps you were fearful for your
life, and you made the tape as evidence.

But it belongs to me now. The truth. The truth about what
you were really doing in a hotel room in L.A. The truth about
why I had to wire you my last five hundred dollars.

It goes like this: There is a prostitute in your room, and
the two of you are snorting cocaine. She makes fun of you because you cannot get hard. "It takes two to tango," she says.

You challenge her. "Don't you like it when I eat you?"

Her response is to worry about the money you owe her.
She charges well over one hundred dollars a night. And
you've been hiring her on a regular basis. Her rent is due. It's
clear that you will have to pay up or face the consequences.

I never asked to know this about you. I never tried to find
out what you really did with my money.

Friends tell me I should blackmail you with the tape. Or
that I should send it to Q105 in Tampa because they will
probably play it on the air. You deserve that sort of public humiliation, some say.

But I firmly believe that meanness begets meanness.
And that Providence did not lead me to the tape so that I
could destroy you. I discovered the tape simply because in

terms of the universe's higher nature, I deserved to know the truth.

Now, let me tell you about my brother and sister and me. We have become honest with one another. So they know all about you. They despise you for what you did to me.

You should also know this. My mother's children have all had a hard time in this life. But we are honorable people. We work hard at being good and happy and productive. We are not always successful. But at least we try. We do not knowingly hurt other people. Astoundingly, we are not bitter. We grapple with our past on a daily basis. But we refuse to allow it to destroy us.

And you know what? Despite all of my parents' faults, I don't blame them for anything. They had tough, sad lives. They fell short so many times. But they weren't evil. They were simply imperfect. Jimmy, Deidre, and I love them to this day.

You should be very glad my parents are dead. If they were alive and knew what you did to me, I believe they would hurt you.

Maybe you will meet them on the other side.

There is one final thing I must tell you.

You did not love my dog.

I do not hold this against you. I do not believe love is part of your nature. But she helped me survive you. And because of that, you must know about her.

Katie went on our honeymoon. She traveled with us

through Texas and New Mexico. She saw the Rancho de Taos and the Pueblo dwellings. She walked on the great sand dunes in Colorado. The fur on the bottom of her paws grew thick in the Kansas cold. And when we returned to Florida, she became an excellent ghost crab hunter. Mika became adept at removing them from her nose.

Her dislike of authority figures never waned. And through the years her grin became wider and a little askew because her teeth began falling out—she was an old dog.

Understand this: She was never unkind. Whenever I cried—whether it was over a movie or hurt feelings or bad memories—she sat on my lap and licked away my tears and stayed by my side until I felt better.

In time, she grew gray and her eyes dim. She lost her hearing, and when we would come into the house after being away, we would gently shake her awake, and she would seem embarrassed that we had caught her napping.

When she was seventeen years old, Katie suffered a stroke. She could no longer walk or eat with ease.

I had always promised her that I would never let her suffer, that I would do all in my power to help her maintain her dignity.

On St. Patrick's Eve 2000, Mika and I made the most gut-wrenching decision of our lives. We put Katie to sleep.

I held her in my arms and I sang to her the Katie song. "K-K-K-Katie, K-K-K-Katie, you're the only d-d-d-dog that I adore. . . ."

Before her final breath, she stretched out in my arms and lifted her head skyward, testing the new air.

We buried her by the sea. The sound of the surf is always with her.

Mika and I will never get over her death. But we try mightily every day to celebrate her life. By loving each other, we honor her. By loving each other, we ascend.

That is all you need to know.